Interfaith Encounter and Dialogue

STUDIEN ZUR INTERKULTURELLEN GESCHICHTE DES CHRISTENTUMS
ETUDES D'HISTOIRE INTERCULTURELLE DU CHRISTIANISME
STUDIES IN THE INTERCULTURAL HISTORY OF CHRISTIANITY

Band 70

Peter Lang
Frankfurt am Main · Bern · New York · Paris

Lynne Price

INTERFAITH ENCOUNTER AND DIALOGUE

A Methodist Pilgrimage

Peter Lang
Frankfurt am Main · Bern · New York · Paris

CIP-Titelaufnahme der Deutschen Bibliothek

Price, Lynne:

Interfaith encounter and dialogue : a Methodist pilgrimage / Lynne Price. - Frankfurt am Main ; Bern ; New York ; Paris : Lang, 1991
(Studien zur interkulturellen Geschichte des Christentums ; Bd. 70)
Zugl.: Birmingham, Univ., Diss., 1989
ISBN 3-631-43735-8

NE: GT

ISSN 0170-9240
ISBN 3-631-43735-8

Printed in Germany 1 3 4 5 6 7

This work is dedicated

TO MY MOTHER

ACKNOWLEDGEMENTS

This book is substantially the text of my thesis "Interfaith Encounter and Dialogue: a positive option or an irrelevance for Methodists in a Religiously Plural Society?" for the degree of Master of Philosophy (Theology) in the University of Birmingham, England, 1989.

I am most grateful to Professor W. J. Hollenweger, who supervised this research, for his guidance and encouragement. It was a privilege to learn with him.

My thanks are given to the minister and members of the church studied for their time and interest and to other friends within and outside Methodism for their helpful contributions.

I also thank my husband Dick, and our children Catherine and Matthew, for their support.

CONTENTS

C O N T E N T S

INTRODUCTION

The lapel badge of Methodism is the Shell of Pilgrimage. The concept of journeying is central to the Christian life, not least because it represents the convergence of apparently polarised values operating in creative tension: purpose and provisionality, security and challenge, openness and commitment. Pilgrimage is essentially participative and dynamic, and as such, is an appropriate image with which to begin consideration of Methodist relations with people of other faiths in Britain.

The question posed is whether interfaith encounter and dialogue is a positive option or an irrelevance for Methodists in a religiously plural society. The question is asked of and from within the tradition, by a Methodist whose experience of encounter with people of other faiths has made it a personal necessity. Further, it is asked by a laywoman, who is by training a social worker, concerned to embrace lay, institutional and theological aspects of the Methodist response. This approach is not without limitations, particularly in the inevitable selectivity required to appraise so broad a spectrum, but was felt necessary in order to facilitate a theological reflection grounded in the practical realities of the situation. It is offered as a contribution to the thinking and practice of the Methodist people, all of whom are priests and missionaries.(1)

Building on the knowledge accumulated in systematic observation and study of religions since the last decades of the nineteenth century, attention is turning increasingly from comparative religion to how the world religions and their adherents relate to each other. David Lochhead suggests that the attitudes adopted by Christianity to other religions could be classified as isolation, hostility, competition or partnership but that none of these is satisfactory because they all "depend on an a priori evaluation of other religious traditions".[2] As an alternative he examines different forms of dialogue (as preparation for conversion, as negotiation, as activity) before selecting "dialogue as relationship" as the "dialogical imperative". Any changes in Christian theology are in this understanding the consequence of dialogue, not a precondition for dialogue.[3] Relation, dialogue and change are the interwoven themes explored in Chapter I, firstly from a global perspective and secondly within the Bible.

Poised, as it were, at a doorway open to the religious thought and experience of the world, through which some traffic has in recent years begun to flow back and forth, we set out to examine the effect of this movement on Methodists and the Methodist Church. The study of a Methodist community in a religiously plural area of Birmingham was carried out from October to November 1988 and doubtless changes will have occurred since; the profile presented is in the nature of a still photograph from a moving film; the intention was to gain some knowledge of how the current situation is viewed by lay Methodists individually and how a local church community functions in relation to its wider community. This information is combined with a review of publications and statements available from The Methodist Church (up to April 1989) regarding relations with people of other faiths. These are collected from a variety of sources within the organizational structure of the institution, reflecting the diversity of issues raised by interfaith dialogue.

Assessment of the present situation prompts the need to understand the ethos of Methodism through its history and development. Three areas are selected - Overseas Mission, Ecumenism and the Doctrine of Christian Perfection - as presenting dominant features of the Methodist tradition which are also held to be significant for relations with people of other faiths. Origins and trends are examined, and recent shifts in thinking and practice noted.

Theological reflection on Methodism and interfaith dialogue finds its place at the end of the present work. Edward Schillebeeckx comments that:

> "by nature the theologian is always 'the latecomer' in respect of Christian practice, which precedes him." (4)

James Dunn and James Mackey, in their book New Testament Theology in Dialogue, make the point that the task of theology is a corporate one, not only within the community of scholarship - they pioneer collaboration between biblical and systematic approaches through case studies on Christology and Church Ministry - but also with the community of faith.[5] Frances Young describes John Wesley as a "link in the chain between the world of the scholar and the ordinary church member"[6] in a book, written with another Methodist, Kenneth Wilson, described as "a plea for Christians and especially ordained ministers, to love God more fully with their minds."[7] Methodism is a newcomer to the discussion on the relationship between Christianity and the other world religions compared with the Roman Catholic and Reformed Churches; its response has been largely to the effect of other religions on its overseas missionary activity since the last century. It has the advantage, therefore, of a freshness of approach, but the disadvantage of little theological resource of its own on which to draw.

Theology and theopraxis are mutually dependent, but their relationship can never achieve a stable equilibrium; their concomitants, reason and experience, vie for the weight of authority in the Methodist tradition.[8] "Theologies", says Wilfred Cantwell Smith, "are conceptual images of God" and cannot be final or complete.[9] We look to Wesley and contemporary Methodists for their contribution to the ongoing process of understanding the God/man/world relationship in the light of their own experience of encounter with other religions.

Our first perspective is that of the world, but as we move inwards into the Methodist tradition the focus changes to the life of the individual Christian. Awareness of the universal and the particular is implicit in all aspects of the study of world religions. Paul Knitter observes:

> "Like all truly great questions, that of the many and the one continues to dog the human spirit, not to lead us to ever new confusions, but to prod us to ever new insights into ourselves, our world and how we are to live our lives." (10)

The differences of perspective are seen as contributing to the understanding of the same scenario; in Martin Buber's thinking:

> "Each man helps bring about the unity of God and the world through genuine dialogue with the created beings among whom he lives. Each man lets God into the world through hallowing the everyday." (11)

-oOo-

References

(1) "The Methodist Church holds the doctrine of the priesthood of all believers" (The Doctrinal Standards, see Appendix B); "the members of the Methodist Missionary Society are the members of the Methodist Church and every member of the Methodist Church as such is a member of the Methodist Missionary Society" (The Constitutional Practice and Discipline of The Methodist Church Vol. 2, pp.679-680).

(2) David Lochhead, The Dialogical Imperative, p.41.

(3) Ibid, Chapter 15, "Dialogue and Theology".

(4) Edward Schillebeeckx, Ministry, p.102; the chapter is entitled "A Brief Hermeneutical Intermezzo".

(5) James D. G. Dunn and James P. Mackey, New Testament Theology in Dialogue, p.22.

(6) Frances Young and Kenneth Wilson, Focus on God, p.44.

(7) Ibid, p.vii of the Preface by John A. Newton.

(8) Ibid, pp.37-45.

(9) Wilfred Cantwell Smith, "Idolatry", in The Myth of Christian Uniqueness, edited by John Hick, p.56.

(10) Paul Knitter, No Other Name?, p.1.

(11) Maurice Friedman, Martin Buber: The Life of Dialogue, p.282.

CHAPTER I

RELATION, DIALOGUE AND CHANGE

1. Contemporary Themes of Change and Convergence

> "Man's religious consciousness as it has emerged over some 70,000 - 80,000 years is too diverse and complex to be synthesized in any set of religious systems deemed to be permanently necessary for man's spiritual development. Religion will always need a climate of openness, diversity and flexibility if it is to respond to the variety of human needs emerging at each new stage of evolution."
> Diarmuid Ó'Murchú (1)

In the twentieth century, technological communications, information processes and means of travel have opened the floodgates of opportunity to explore, learn from and relate to the richness of the world's people, cultures and environments. Knowledge and experience of the world and its people is now not only more abundant and more widely available but also becoming understood in an immediate and specific way: the parts are dynamically and incontrovertibly part of the whole. Through the apparent diversity and fragmentation there may be seen to be emerging an affective, experiential and spiritual sense of commonality, of a shared Earth and a shared humanity. The major global phenomena of the pollution of the planet and possibility of nuclear war, which threaten the maintenance and continuance of life, bring into sharp awareness the need for salvific action. The ecological movement, the peace movement, the New Age Teachings, the growing adoption of meditation practices, the interest in holistic medicine and spiritual healing are all evidence of this awareness of a new sense of unity and purpose.

Study of the physical and biological sciences, sociology, social anthropology, psychology and other related disciplines has become highly developed in western cultures, all contributing from different perspectives to observation, understanding of and insight into the 'human condition'. More recently signs of convergence are emerging from independent disciplines and interdisciplinary studies. In the area of the physical sciences, for example, Peter Russell[2] draws particularly on the Gaia Hypothesis of the chemist Dr. James Lovelock, which postulates that our planet behaves like a living system. Tracing the evolutionary trend towards increasing complexity and organisation, Russell then demonstrates how

> "theoretical physics is paying considerable attention to the way in which the many varied phenomena of the Universe appear to be but manifestations of a single underlying whole."(3)

He comments:

> "Even though these theories are coming from physicists, they are beginning to sound more and more like the teachings of the mystics. Indeed, if the Universe is ultimately a unity we should expect such a convergence of ideas."(4)

Moving from the realm of the global to the personal, Carl Gustav Jung, through his meticulous observation and psychotherapeutic work with his patients (and his extensive knowledge of comparative religion and mythology and travels in Africa and North America), came to distinguish three psychic levels: consciousness, the personal unconscious and the collective unconscious. Consequently, not only is individual mental health viewed as unity of the personality, but the <u>collective unconscious</u>:

"as the ancestral heritage of possibilities of representation is not individual but common to all men, and perhaps even to all animals, and is the true basis of the individual psyche." (5)

In Psychology and Religion he carries this postulation of an underlying, common human unity into statements that "the ordinary man, too, unconsciously lives archetypal forms" and "Ultimately, every individual life is at the same time the eternal life of the species."(6) A fuller discussion of Carl Jung and global consciousness can be found in Ó'Murchú's Coping With Change in the Modern World.(7) He comments:

"Jungian psychology and classical mysticism are remarkably similar in the global vision, one they share today with an increasing number of scientific disciplines." (8)

Paul Knitter comments on Jung:

"From his discoveries of the unconscious and the presence of the God-image within it, Jung drew conclusions concerning the nature of the established religions, their differences and their similarities. His conclusions aid many today in making sense of the reality of religious pluralism." (9)

Teilhard de Chardin, palaeontologist, biologist and Jesuit, during the same period as Jung, (Jung 1875-1961, de Chardin 1881-1955), had through evolutionary studies similarly arrived at observations of change and convergence.(10) He envisaged a new era of evolution ('noogenesis'): the physical development of the human species having been almost completed means that further growth would take place in the realm of the spiritual. In a lecture given in 1943 he says:

"The mankind of tomorrow is emerging from the mists of the future, and we can actually see it taking shape: a 'super-mankind', much more conscious, much more powerful, and much more unanimous than our own. And at the same time .... we can detect an underlying but deeply rooted feeling that if we are to reach the ultimate of our own selves, we must do more than link our own being with a handful of other beings selected from the thousands that surround us:

> we must form one whole with all simultaneously. .....
> Awaiting us is a centre of a higher order - and already we can distinguish it - not simply beside us, but beyond and above us." (11)

It is worthy of observation that the psychologist and the biologist whom we have selected to illustrate the theme of change and convergence are each, from their own disciplines and through their own experience, centrally concerned with spiritual development: Carl Jung revealed explicitly in his autobiography the driving force of his life's work:

> "One must be utterly abandoned to God; nothing matters but fulfilling His will. Otherwise all is folly and meaningless. From that moment on, when I experienced grace, my true responsibility began." (12)

Teilhard de Chardin's contribution is summed up by Sir Julian Huxley in his introduction to The Phenomenon of Man thus:

> "Through his combination of wide scientific knowledge with deep religious feeling and a rigorous sense of values, he has forced theologians to view their ideas in the new perspective of evolution, and scientists to see the spiritual implications of their knowledge." (13)

Neither were, during their lifetimes, esteemed by the established churches or established scholarship: it is only since their deaths that their contributions to the religious history of the century have been reluctantly recognised. Their respective works are in themselves exemplary of convergence - of observing, evaluating and absorbing knowledge and insights from disciplines other than theology into a fuller understanding of God and the World.

Signs of convergence are, perhaps, most tangibly recognisable in the changed and changing nature of the societies in which we live. Long-term or permanent migration, although by no means a new phenomenon in world history, has been most notable in its pattern of movement from East to West in this century. Indian, Bangladeshi and Pakistani migrants to Britain have settled and the communities developing from them are now an established part of the indigenous population. Groups of 'guest workers' from Turkey living in Germany and Sweden and migrants from North Africa to France are other examples of this movement in recent decades. The meeting of religions and cultures in our pluralist societies may be seen for the purposes of this research to be the most practical stimulus for interfaith dialogue and encounter.

According to Kevin Walcot, of the Catholic missionary Society of the Divine Word, migration by members of other religions to pluralist societies will diminish the likelihood of conversion to Christianity because the need for group identity (sociologically and religiously) will increase. In global terms he draws attention to the fact that there is now little opportunity for people to be converted from primal religions as they have already been converted to one of the major world religions. He understands the modern missionary task as that of dialogue to develop contacts between Christian believers and the world religions.[14]

This brief and selective attempt to identify some of the distinguishing elements of "our time" sets the contemporary context for the question, 'should interfaith dialogue and encounter be an important focus of thought, prayer and action for Christian theology, the Christian Church and individual Christians?' In addressing the question 'why now?' it becomes apparent that the scene has already been set on the world stage, (awareness of a shared Earth and common humanity), the props gathered (knowledge, reflective consciousness, technology) and the actors assembled (pluralist societies).

Interfaith dialogue and encounter can consequently be viewed as a response to the events and needs of the age, rather than an initiative. Teilhard de Chardin's concept of Christianity's force towards the Transcendant (Faith in God) and human force towards an Immanent (Faith in Man) resulting in a 'super-humanised' Christian faith,(15) can be taken as an inspiration for effort in the area of interfaith dialogue and encounter. Knitter comments:

> "The world religions are confronting each other as never before and they are experiencing a new sense of identity and purpose because they, like atoms and humans and cultures, are moving towards a more pervasive unity through better relationships with each other. They are being urged by what seems to be the creative lure within all reality toward a new form of unity, a unitive pluralism." (16)

It is suggested within the context of convergence and unity of our shared world and common humanity, now becoming clearly identified by the physical and social sciences, (together with all the pain, tension and conflict involved in this unity becoming a reality), that theology, the institutional Church and individual Christians - interrelatedly, not as separate entities - have both to contribute to, and receive from, the processes and outcomes of dialogue and encounter as part of this movement. Movement, as Diarmuid Ó'Murchú, a Roman Catholic priest and social psychologist, points out in the quotation with which we began this chapter, is necessary for man's spiritual development.

2. Encounter and Dialogue in the Bible

(a) "In the beginning is relation" (17)

The Scriptural presentation of God's first encounter with man is in the story of Creation; it is the meeting between God and man on the basis of a relationship - that of the Creator to the created. No sooner had God created Adam in the world and told him, "You may eat freely of every tree of the garden; but of the tree of the knowledge of good and evil you shall not eat, for in the day that you eat of it you shall die" (Gen. 2:15), than Adam and Eve, having disobeyed, are called to explain why and life is made difficult for them. But they do not die 'in the day' and God provides them with protection for their new environment ("And the Lord God made for Adam and his wife garments of skins, and clothed them", Gen. 3:21). God, the universal Creator is perceived as maintaining a continuing relationship with humanity. The medium in which this understanding is conveyed is that of dialogue and was the outcome, according to Von Rad, of six or seven centuries of Israel's experience and understanding of the saving Acts of God in her history. It was on the basis of Israel's relationship with God that the later writers embraced and adapted the prevailing myths of other cultures. He points out that the accounts of Creation given by the Jahwist (Genesis 11) and the Priestly Document (Genesis 1) view creation "as a prologue, and as a start of the divine saving work in Israel". Whether accepted as a literal reality or the product of theological reflection, the story of Creation speaks of the on-going relationship between God and man.(18)

Our contemporary global perspective of shared world and common humanity can be interpreted as a rediscovery of that which was clearly grasped by the writer of the story of Noah and the universal covenant: all the people and living creatures of the earth are descended from the inhabitants of the Ark.

> "I will never again curse the ground because of man, for the imagination of man's heart is evil from his youth; neither will I ever again destroy every living creature as I have done. While the earth remains, seedtime and harvest, cold and heat, summer and winter, day and night, shall not cease" (Gen. 8:21-22).

The rainbow is the sign of the covenant "which I make between me and you and every living creature that is with you, for all future generations" (Gen. 9:12). It is an all-embracing and "everlasting" bond.

The further and particular aspects of the God/man relationship are explored throughout the Old Testament. The account in Genesis 18:16 - 19:29) of Abraham "interceding" with God when He makes known His possible intention to destroy Sodom because of its wickedness, is marked by a detailed and lengthy debate. Perhaps the most striking aspect is that God is presented by the author as coming to a decision to tell Abraham of his intention:

> "Shall I hide from Abraham what I am about to do, seeing that Abraham shall become a great and mighty nation, and all the nations of the earth shall bless themselves by him? No, for I have chosen him, that he may charge his children and his household after him to keep the way of the Lord by doing righteousness and justice;" (Gen 18:17-19).

Abraham's response is no less surprising. He challenges God:

> "Wilt thou indeed destroy the righteous with the wicked? Far be it from thee to do such a thing, to slay the righteous with the wicked, so that the righteous fare as the wicked! Far be that from thee! Shall not the Judge of all the earth do right?" (Gen. 18:23, 25.)

Erich Fromm sees in this episode an important change in the concept of God which has resulted from the covenant made with Noah and reaffirmed with Abraham (Gen. 17:1-14):

> "Abraham challenges God not by disobedience but by accusing him of violating his own promises and principles." (19)

The outcome of the story is that God saves Lot and his daughters and destroys Sodom and Gomorrah. Abraham did not know this when he embarked on the debate: he emerged from it with a better understanding of how God acts in the world, but whether he influenced the outcome is open to question. There are parallels to be drawn here when we address contemporary inter-faith dialogue. The possibility of dialogue is conditional upon the nature of the relationship between those participating. When God, with his two companions, appears to Abraham, Abraham's response is to offer them service and food, and when they are ready to leave he goes with them to "set them on their way". There is a wholeness of body, mind and spirit in the offering and acceptance of rest and refreshment before the consideration of righteousness, wickedness and punishment, which underpins the ensuing dialogue. Revelation is depicted as touching all aspects of what it means to be human.

The prophets are intrinsic elements in the dialogue of revelation: they reveal the God of history to the people (e.g. Isaiah 13:1 - 14:27 concerning Babylon; Isaiah 22:1-25 concerning Jerusalem); they make clear the way God wants them to act (e.g. Micah 6:8 "He has showed you, O man, what is good: and what does the Lord require of you but to do justice, and to love kindness, and to walk humbly with your God?"). The prophets show man the alternatives between which they can choose and the consequences of the choice (e.g. Samuel 8:4-22 - the people want a king but Samuel is against it; God explains to Samuel why they are making this request and tells him to warn the people what will happen if they have a king. Samuel takes their response back to God and is told to "make them a king"). Not only is the prophet a messenger between God and the people, he also participates in the action. The prophets are sometimes depicted as the mouthpiece of God (e.g. Jeremiah 1:7, "But the Lord said to me, 'Do not say, "I am only a youth"; for to all to whom I send you you shall go, and whatever I command you you shall speak'"; Ezekiel 2:7 "And you shall speak my words to them, whether they hear or refuse to hear; for they are a rebellious house".) The prophets' claims to understand and interpret God's will and action are on the basis of their relationship to the communities of which they are part. History is not an event to be observed, it is a process in which they are involved; a process which Von Rad points out, is "open to the future" in that Israel, through a variety of traditions represented in different narrative forms, saw herself "poised between promise and fulfilment".[20]

> "Meeting with God does not come to man in order that he may concern himself with God, but in order that he may confirm that there is meaning in the world." (21)

Martin Buber's "world of relation" is built in three spheres: our life with nature (Cosmos), our life with men (Eros) and our life with spiritual beings (Logos).[22] All three are characterised by two attitudes - "I-Thou" and "I-It"; life consists in relationships in the I-Thou attitude, but as experiences in the I-It attitude.[23] It is the "between" of God, people and nature which is both vital and common.

> "In every sphere in its own way, through each process of becoming that is present to us we look out toward the fringe of the eternal _Thou_; in each we are aware of a breath from the eternal _Thou_; in each _Thou_ we address the eternal _Thou_." (24)

In the sphere of life with men:

> "_I_ and _Thou_ take their stand not merely in relation, but also in the solid give-and-take of talk. ... The relation with man is the real simile of the relation with God; in it true address receives true response; except that in God's response everything, the universe, is made manifest in language." (25)

Significance for the purposes of the present study is also seen in that Martin Buber as a Hebrew scholar has been able to address the issues that concern Jews and Christians in a way that is meaningful to both. Vision beyond perceived boundaries characterises convergence, encounter and revelation: it becomes shared through relationship and evidenced in the "solid give-and-take of talk". The view that religion is essentially concerned with the nature of relationship between God, the natural world and human beings is fundamental to the approach of this research.

John Robinson is akin to Martin Buber when he says:

> "Statements about God are acknowledgements of the transcendent, unconditional element in all our relationships, and supremely in our relationships with other persons." (26)

There is no basis for assuming that "other persons" means 'other Christians' or that in trying to be "Honest to God" we should not also try to be 'Honest to People'. In theology as well as in theopraxis we should be open to the knowledge that our deepest relationships with people of other faiths also acknowledge the transcendent and unconditional.

(b) <u>The Pattern of the Ministry of Jesus</u>

According to Matthew's Gospel, after his baptism and temptation Jesus began to preach: "Repent, for the kingdom of heaven is at hand." An eminent Methodist minister once clarified 'to repent' as 'to sit loose'.[27]. This could be taken as the keynote of Jesus' ministry - 'Change! - a new way of life is available'. This is followed by the summons to Peter and Andrew, "Follow me, and I will make you fishers of men." The encounter of command and mission with looking and listening results in change: "immediately they left their nets and followed him".

Jesus' whole ministry could be said to be one of dialogue and encounter. He moves around, preaching in synagogues, teaching to groups of people who gather round him in the countryside, healing people who stop him in the streets. Jesus makes himself available; he utilizes situations (e.g Luke 6:6-11, Jesus went to the synagogue to preach; "a man was there whose right hand was withered" who becomes the focus of discussion about understanding the purpose of the Sabbath); he responds to individuals ("a leper came to him and knelt before him saying, 'Lord, if you will, you can make me clean'. And he stretched out his hand and touched him, saying, 'I will; be clean'", Mat. 8:2-3). No preconditions are laid down for encounter, it arises from relation, the "between" of knowledge and love.[28] "When he saw the crowds he had compassion for them, because they were harassed and helpless, like sheep without a shepherd" (Mat. 9:36).

Jesus' method of teaching by parables often gave rise to the need for elucidation (e.g. "Explain to us the parable of the weeds of the field," Mat.13:36). "Have you understood all this?" Jesus asks after a series of parables about the kingdom of heaven (Mat. 13:51). Jesus accepts that those listening to him have varying levels of understanding. Stories mean different things in different situations to different people, but this is a measure of their intrinsic validity: it means they have to be applied with individual understanding in particular situations - they have to be experienced to be fully understood.

Jesus was a master of using participation as a means of communication - his own as well as that of his hearers. The episode recorded in Luke 7:36-50 is a rich tapestry of encounter, involvement, questioning, dialogue and observation. Simon the Pharisee invites Jesus to his home for a meal and while he is there a "woman of the city, who was a sinner" washed Jesus' feet with tears, dried them with her hair and anointed them. A pillar of the establishment, a dubious new preacher, a prostitute, the assembled company - a tense situation topped by an extravagant display of love and devotion! Jesus speaks: "Simon, I have something to say to you." "What is it, Teacher?" And Jesus tells a story about writing off debts on which he asks Simon's opinion. Jesus confirms his answer and then uses the behaviour of the woman to point to the relation between love and forgiveness. This initiates fresh questions about Jesus' authority. There is an interweaving of many elements in the dialogue and encounter between Jesus and those present: formal religious attitudes, love in action, issues of ethics and values, new perspectives, criticism, dynamic relationships, compassionate insight and disgruntled muttering and hostility. We shall find all these same elements when we turn our attention to contemporary inter-faith dialogue.

Encounter was frequently initiated by other people: "And, behold, a lawyer stood up to put him to the test, saying, 'Teacher, what shall I do to inherit eternal life?'" (Luke 10:25-37) Jesus meets the man where he is: "What is written in the law? How do you read?" - 'What do _you_ think?' The lawyer quotes the Great Commandments. 'You are right', confirms Jesus, but the lawyer presses a further question: "And who is my neighbour?" Jesus answers with a story, rather than a statement. Stories, as we have said, are open to interpretation, and this one has a subtle twist which demands a change in direction. As Walter Hollenweger points out, the answer changes the question from 'who is my neighbour?' to 'who loved the victim?'[29] Words of Dietrich Bonhoeffer come to mind:

> "We come to a clearer and more sober estimate of our own limitations and responsibilities, and that makes it possible for us genuinely to love our neighbours. So long as we are suffering from an exaggerated sense of our own importance we can never really love our neighbours;" (30)

The episode demonstrates superbly the dynamics of encounter and dialogue: the lawyer puts Jesus "to the test" of the Torah; Jesus understands that the man is presenting the whole of his way of life for comment, and enters a relationship with him on the basis of what he believes and practises; Jesus recognises what the lawyer brings to the situation and concurs with his answer. A further question proceeds from a common foundation in a manner which invites exploration and discovery on the part of the questioner. The lawyer is led beyond the legalistic definition of who qualifies for neighbourliness to the nature of love and loving. As we observed in Abraham's debate with God about the fate of Sodom, outcomes of dialogue are unknown, whether they take place with the being who is perceived as God or, in the case of the lawyer, a man who is perceived as a new local Jewish preacher called Jesus. This raises another issue relating to partners in dialogue: it was not necessary for the lawyer to hold any set of beliefs about Jesus (that he was the Messiah, the Son of God etc.) in order to enter a dialogical relationship with him - or, indeed, to benefit from it. Neither was he required to abandon his loyalty to Torah.

There are lessons to be learnt from the style and manner of Jesus' ministry found in the Synoptic Gospels which apply to inter-faith dialogue and encounter. He was not promulgating the establishment of a new religion or reform of the Jewish synagogues. Jesus was promulgating a new way of living for men and women which demanded a shift in perception and attitude resulting in true self-awareness, and a qualitatively different relationship with God and with other people. "You shall love the Lord your God with all your heart, and with all your soul, and with all your strength, and with all your mind; and your neighbour as yourself". "You have answered right; do this, and you will live" (Luke 10:27, 28).

(c) Dialogue and Encounter in the Early Christian Community

> "The Christian Church is built round the post-Easter kerygma, not the teaching of the historical Jesus." (31)

> "When frontiers are crossed, when new dimensions of faith are discovered - above all when this is in contradiction to hitherto dearly-held principles - it seems that quarrel in the church is inevitable. That was already the case in the original Christian community." (32)

The rapid shift from the God-centred ministry of Jesus to the Jesus-centred ministry of the early church in the light of his death, resurrection and the events of Pentecost created a state of turmoil in which the Church continues to reel. Paul alludes very little to the teachings of Jesus in his letters and the growing groups of believers soon feel the need to get organised - allocating responsibilities and creating social structures. Tensions between 'sending' and 'gathering' functions emerge. Roles have to be defined - for men and women, freemen and slaves, Jews and non-Jews; the nature of authority has to be clarified - initially resting with the apostles on the basis of their unique relationship to the earthly Jesus, but being given a new perspective by Paul, who had not known him, who sees it as conditional upon both tradition and Spirit. As James Dunn points out:

> "the authoritative expression of preaching or teaching in any particular case takes the form of interpreted tradition." (33)

We remind ourselves that the Christian 'tradition' was largely oral and that what had been written at this time remained fragmentary; much of the New Testament canon did not exist and the Nicene Creed was more than two centuries away. Spirit and experience were the order of the day.(34) Dialogue, debate and, indeed, conflict were the inevitable consequences of diversity. Schillebeeckx directs us to "the dangerous and creative recollection of the necessary unity in tension between charisma and institutionalisation in referring to this period."(35)

The most prominent and far-reaching dialogue in the early church arose from the question of whether the Gospel was for anyone other than Jews. In the account in Acts 10, the story does not begin with the Christian community (centred in Jerusalem) but at Caesarea with Cornelius, "a devout man who feared God with all his household, gave alms liberally to the people, and prayed constantly to God" (Acts 10.1-2); he receives a vision telling him to send for Peter. That God was at work outside Judaism was probably not a new concept to Peter, but to actually acknowledge it in practice by 'getting his hands dirty' took a visionary experience and a definite change in the way he viewed non-Jews. Addressing Cornelius and his household and friends, Peter says, "You yourselves know how unlawful it is for a Jew to associate with or to visit any one of another nation; but God has shown me that I should not call any man common or unclean" (Acts 10:28). Peter preaches the gospel to them and before he has finished, (he is quoted by Luke as saying, "as I began to speak" when giving his account later, Acts 11:15), "the Holy Spirit fell on all who heard the word" (Acts 10:44); they were heard "speaking in tongues and extolling God" (Acts 10:46). Walter Hollenweger makes the point:

> "The real evangelist cannot help but take the risk that in the course of his evangelism his understanding of Christ will get corrected." (36)

Further than this, attention might be drawn to the declared motivating force of this evangelistic enterprise - God: "Truly

I perceive that God shows no partiality, but in every nation any one who fears him and does what is right is acceptable to him."

Peter, through encounter with God (vision) and reflection on his own attitudes and prejudices, enters a relationship with Cornelius and his household characterised by shared respect and equality before God. In his mind is allegiance to Jewish ritual cleanliness and superiority, but he is inexorably drawn by the events towards the recognition of inner purity and commonality. His own conflict resolved, he is then called to explain himself back at headquarters in Jerusalem. The account in Acts 11:1-8 tells us Peter simply told the apostles and brethren what had happened, and appeals: "If then God gave the same gift to them as he gave to us when we believed in the Lord Jesus Christ, who was I that I could withstand God?" There was nothing more to be said!

But there was: the flashlight of truth also casts shadows. There were already, according to Dunn, schisms in the early church in Jerusalem evidenced by Stephen's attitude to the Temple and the Hellenistic widows being missed out of the distribution of the common fund.(37) Now the question could not be avoided of whether non-Jewish Christians were bound by Torah. Paul and Barnabas take up the anti-circumcision lobby and contribute with the elders to the reaching of an agreement (Acts 15:1-35; Gal. 2:1-10).(38) Barriers to the work among the non-Jews had been removed, but the practicalities had not been fully addressed: uneasy compromise remained despite the expression of solidarity made by the Christians outside Israel taking and sending a collection for the poor in Jerusalem.

In the coming together of different cultures and traditions which was to be a feature of Paul's ministry, seemingly endless subjects of debate came up, highlighted in the day-to-day difficulties of a mixed group of people trying to live and worship together, as in Corinth,(39) as much as in the theological manoeuvering needed to preach the gospel meaningfully to different communities, as in Paul using the statue to the unknown God in Athens to identify the Universal Creator "in whom we live and move and have our being" (Acts 17:22-32).

The issues may change, but the debate continues. Circumcision is no longer an issue among Christians, but the sharing and administration of Communion, for example, is. Inter-cultural theology is now making serious attempts in the post-colonial era to share the perceptions and insights of non-western Christians in adapting and adopting what is already in existence in their communities and traditions.(40) The philosophy of language is increasing our understanding of how words and ideas are to be understood in their cultural contexts. We learn to recognise meaningful connecting points in the hopes and needs of others (Christian participation in peace and ecology groups). To borrow Walter Hollenweger's phrase, "the Good News is in the making".(41)

> "to risk our understanding of the Good News belongs to the goodness of that Good News because its goodness does not depend on our understanding of it." (42)

3. Summary

The stimulus for encounter, relation and dialogue with people of other religions is to be found in the contemporary movement towards convergence resulting in a new global perception of shared Earth and common humanity. This is manifest in interdisciplinary understandings of the God/natural world/humanity configuration and made possible by man's evolutionary and technological progress. The significant growth of pluralist societies in Britain lends further immediacy to the responsibility of theologians, the churches and individual Christians to rethink and react to their role in God's purpose.

The firm basis for renewed effort and the source of energy is seen in God's relationship with humanity - *all* people - revealed in the myths and stories of the Old Testament, interpreted as meaningful by the authors and accepted as having the authority of Scripture by Christians. It is God's encounter and continuing relationship with man which stimulates dialogue and activity in understanding and implementing His purpose for the world. *I-Thou* rather than *I-It* attitudes between people, and between people and the natural world, are reflections of God's relationship with people.

The pattern of the life and teaching of Jesus in the Synoptic Gospels is our example and guide in our Christian relations with other people. We have particularly emphasized the method of encounter and dialogue which Jesus so often used, which was indicative of the nature of his relationship with those around him and with God. He took people - fishermen, lawyers, prostitutes - seriously and responded both to their need and their potential for change. He loved them.

For those who grasped the importance of Jesus, his life took on new meaning in the further events of his death, resurrection and the outpouring of the Holy Spirit on the day of Pentecost. The understanding, interpretation and formulation of the Gospel evolved during the evangelistic process and became formalised, though not completed, in the establishment of a church structure. The early anticipated second coming of the risen Jesus did not materialise; diversity and dialogue continued and is exemplified today by a plethora of Christian denominations and rapid rise in new religious movements.

The Good News is, indeed, in the making: its development may be best discerned by the rediscovery, in our own time, of the world of relation which the Bible reveals to us and which we are called to give meaning to. Our relationships with people of other faiths are, therefore, set firmly in humanity's relation to God as the Universal Creator and Sustainer, illuminated by the ministry of Jesus and inspired by the early Christian community, which followed where God led and, struggling with the consequences, hoped for an ultimate solution. The diversity of interpretation, belief and practice amongst the world religions of the movement towards a different state of being human is held together in the fundamental unity of humanity in a shared world and the hope of something better at the end.

Paragraph 19 of the Statement adopted by the Theological Consultation on "Dialogue in Community" held at Chiang Mai, April 1977 says :

> "In dialogue we actively respond to the command 'to love God and your neighbour as yourself'."

Paragraph 21 adds:

> "We should think always in terms of people of other faiths and ideologies rather than of theoretical, impersonal systems." (43)

Inter-faith encounter is a way of learning to live the Great Commandments. We have as much to gain as to offer - but only if we are willing to change, to be made new and to participate in a qualitatively new way of living in relation to God, the world and people.

> "The Christian churches are in danger of undermining the central message of the New Testament, in danger too of shielding their members from the vital challenge of God's word. The renewed call of every generation is to be a leaven, fresh dough, a people who will bring alive with new intensity God's message and its invitation to action in the context of each new era." (44)

-oOo-

References

(1) Diarmuid Ó'Murchú, The God Who Becomes Redundant, pp.157-8.

(2) Peter Russell, The Awakening Earth; pp.7-10 on the Gaia Hypothesis; Chapter 3 on "Hidden Orders in Evolution".

(3) Ibid, pp.124-128.

(4) Ibid, p.127.

(5) Carl Gustav Jung, The Structure of the Psyche, Collected Works 8, paras. 317-21. Quoted from Anthony Storr Jung: Selected Writings, p.67.

(6) Carl Gustav Jung, Psychology and Religion, Collected Works 11, paras. 138-49 in Selected Writings, p.248.

(7) Diarmuid Ó'Murchú, Coping With Change in the Modern World, pp.96-107.

(8) Ibid, p. 107.

(9) Paul Knitter, No Other Name?, p.60.

(10) Teilhard de Chardin, The Phenomenon of Man.

(11) Teilhard de Chardin, Toward the Future, p.120.

(12) Carl Gustav Jung, Memories, Dreams, Reflections, p.57.

(13) Teilhard de Chardin, The Phenomenon of Man, pp.27-28.

(14) Kevin Walcot, SVD, "Redefining the Boundaries of Mission? Challenges ahead for missionary societies", Verbum SVD, Fasciculus 1, Volumen 29, 1988, pp.3-10.

(15) Teilhard de Chardin, The Future of Man, pp.272-282.

(16) Paul Knitter, op. cit., p.9.

(17) Martin Buber, I and Thou, p.32.

(18) Gerhard von Rad, Old Testament Theology, Vol. I, pp.136-140.

(19) Erich Fromm, You Shall Be As Gods, p.28. Fromm interprets this as a stage in man's liberation from God; Abraham relates to God as a free man party to an agreement.

(20) Gerhard Von Rad, Old Testament Theology, Vol.II, p.414.

(21) Martin Buber, I and Thou, p.147.

(22) Ibid, pp.18-19, 130-131.

(23) Ibid, pp.15-18.

(24) Ibid, p.19.

(25) Ibid, p.132.

(26) John A. T. Robinson, Honest to God, p.52.

(27) Rev. C. Hughes Smith, verbal communication July 1986.

(28) Martin Buber, op. cit., p.111.

(29) Walter J. Hollenweger, Evangelism Today: Good News or Bone of Contention?, p.78.

(30) Dietrich Bonhoeffer, op. cit., p.89.

(31) James Dunn, Unity and Diversity in the New Testament, p.32.

(32) Walter J. Hollenweger, *op. cit.*, p.15.

(33) James Dunn, *op. cit.*, p.78.

(34) *Ibid*, pp. 174-202.

(35) Edward Schillebeeckx, *Ministry: A case for change*; p.24.

(36) Walter Hollenweger, *op. cit.*, p.17.

(37) James Dunn, *op. cit.*, pp.268-275.

(38) For a discussion of the Apostolic Conference, see Ferdinand Hahn, *Mission in the New Testament*, pp.77-86.

(39) See Walter Hollenweger, *Conflict in Corinth* for narrative exegetical presentation of the tensions in the early Christian community.

(40) See, for example, C. Nyamiti, *Christ as our Ancestor*.

(41) Walter Hollenweger, *Evangelism Today: Good News or Bone of Contention?*, p.94.

(42) *Ibid*, p.95.

(43) S. J. Samartha, (ed.) *Faith in the Midst of Faiths*, pp.144, 145.

(44) Diarmuid Ó'Murchú, *Coping With Change in the Modern World*, p.211.

CHAPTER II

FROM PEW TO CONFERENCE

Methodist Relations with People of Other Faiths in Britain

Having begun in the global dimensions of shared world and common humanity before examining the Judaeo/Christian Biblical foundation for dialogical relationships in humanity's religious quest, we now turn our attention to the specific area of interest: the nature of British Methodism's relations with other faiths. Bearing in mind the World Council of Churches statement that we should think in terms of people of other faiths rather than of theoretical systems, we begin by observing how ordinary lay members of a Methodist community in Birmingham are responding to being Christians amongst people of other religions. Section 2 examines how the awareness of religious pluralism is affecting thinking and policy formation within the institutional structure of Methodism and Section 3 notes the statements of the Methodist Church on Faith and Order regarding "Other Faiths".

1. Study of a Methodist Church in a Religiously Plural Area of Birmingham

The purpose of the Study

The purpose of the Study was to ascertain how members of a Methodist community situated in a religiously plural area describe and understand their relation to members of non-Christian religious communities (Hindus, Sikhs, Muslims, Jews, Buddhists).

Selection of a Church

The criteria set for selection were i) a Methodist Church; ii) located in a multi-faith and multi-racial area of Birmingham; iii) having a minister interested in multi-faith issues and willing to give some time to the researcher.

The Chairman of the Birmingham District of the Methodist Church was contacted to invite his comment on the intended study. His positive support led him to suggest four possible churches which might meet the criteria set. One was chosen by the researcher and the minister contacted. This was followed by a meeting with the minister at which a full discussion of the researcher's work took place, consideration was given to the draft questionnaire and the minister supplied information about the church community. The minister agreed to put the matter to Church Council. No difficulties were presented to the implementation of the study.

The Church and its Environment

The church itself, built in 1915, is a large, imposing, red-brick edifice facing a busy main road which is scattered with blocks of terraced houses, a school, small businesses and a wide variety of small shops, many with goods displayed on the pavements. Much of the area has been subject to the Local Authority's Urban Renewal Programme and the houses are structurally sound and well maintained. Metal and mesh shields protect the stained-glass windows of the church: a few modest pieces of graffiti adorn one wall, in some way highlighting the sturdy and cared-for character of the church. The rear adjoins one side of a long, immaculate road of pre-First World War terraced houses, neatly walled and gated, with many of the original decorative windows preserved. New pavements shaped to define car parking areas emphasize the orderliness of the litter-free road. The uniformity is punctuated at intervals by hanging baskets of flowers and trellissed plants. Observation of pedestrians passing the church suggests a white, Asian and Afro-Caribbean population in equal proportions. The 1981 Census figures confirm that over half the people in the ward lived in households with the head born in the New Commonwealth or Pakistan. There is also a local Vietnamese community.

The premises are extensive and offer themselves to a variety of uses. A small room by the entrance to the church hall is rented to a government-sponsored help agency. An additional chapel was built in 1923 and stands adjacent to the church. It is rented to a black Pentecostal church for services on Sunday mornings and evenings, and on one evening a week to a local choral society. Another room is rented on Sunday afternoons and evenings to a second black church group. Adjoining the front of the small chapel is a self contained set of rooms on two floors which are let to an outside government-funded agency offering work training to women. The director is a Hindu woman, born in India, and the all-female staff are of mixed ethnic and religious groups. The implementation of this arrangement was due largely to the commitment of the minister (in gaining support of the Church Council) and the Property Steward (who dealt with the administration and alterations to the building in conjunction with the Property Division): no church members are involved with the project. Again through the initiative of the minister and the co-operation of the director of the project, effort is being made to ascertain the needs in the area for full-time playgroup facilities. The Church playgroup at present is not well subscribed and lacking in volunteers from the church to staff it.

Cub, Scout and Brownie groups function under the auspices of the church, only the Brownies being run by a member of the church. Most of the children who attend are not from church families and attempts on the part of the minister to re-institute Parade Services are proving difficult. Such services would provide the only contact between the Cub and Scout groups and the church congregation. The Brownie leader is an effective line of communication between her group and the church (the Brownies have taken part in the occasional Family Services and the Carol Service) and welcomes girls of all ethnic and religious backgrounds to the pack (at present there are none, though there have been Hindu and Sikh girls). Her position has led her to take an interest in other religions through reading and television programmes and to think through the implications of the Brownie Promise "To do my duty to God" for a multi-faith group. The girls have been encouraged to think about what this means in their own faiths, and the closing prayers referred to God rather than Jesus.

The young people's group which used to meet for discussions, videos etc on Sunday afternoons at the manse has changed its composition as teenagers have drifted away.

The weekly lunch club is the 'outreach' activity in which most time and energy is invested by the largest group of church members. A rota of cooks, servers, washers-up and car-drivers provides an excellent lunch at a reasonable cost in a friendly atmosphere for 25-35 elderly members and their friends. It is in principle open to anybody, but in practice is attended (and administered) by white Christians. It was thought that no black church people were involved because they were virtually all younger and at work (this is certainly true of the participants in the study). Language difficulties and differences in food-tastes were given as reasons why no people from other ethnic or religious groups attended.

The three other regular weekly meetings - the Wesley Guild, the Womens Group and the Fellowship/Bible study group serve the church community. The latter group, led by the minister, has had some discussion on other religions.

The membership roll stands at 157 and there are many more people on the 'community roll'. The average attendance at morning service is 90 - 100 and the evening fluctuates between 15 and 30. In the winter months the evening service is moved to 3.30 pm. Slightly more than a third of members are of Afro-Caribbean origin or descent and this ratio is reflected in the morning congregations. The average age of the black members of this Methodist community is lower than that of the white members, most of whom are retired. Only a handful of people in their teens and early twenties attend and the Sunday School has a weekly attendance of 8 - 12 children, including babies.

The church belongs to a circuit of eight churches, with four Ministers, two Pastoral Assistants, a Youth and Community Worker and thirteen local preachers. Few joint circuit events take place and the Pastoral Assistants and Youth and Community Worker are attached to other churches.

Ecumenical Involvement

United services are held during the Autumn, Lent and Holy Week with the local Anglican, Roman Catholic and United Reformed churches. Joint activities are now in their third successful year, having developed from clerical initiatives taken up by a council. Shared participation in Lent Groups, combined meetings during Holy Week and a joint procession of witness on Good Friday culminating in an open-air service to which each denomination contributes are examples of co-operative effort. Joint ecumenical services are held at regular intervals throughout the year. At least one of the Lent Groups has continued to meet 'unofficially' as members have found personal enrichment from sharing their traditions.

The four churches have combined again for the second year to provide Christmas lunch, entertainment, carols and tea for any members and friends who wish to share together in this way and particularly the elderly and others who might be alone. The premises of our study church are used for this truly co-operative and successful venture, which approximately 62 people attended in 1988, including a Muslim mother and daughter.

The church, through its minister, participates in a monthly forum of churches (black- and white-led) situated in adjacent local authority wards and which is attended mainly by clergy and also interested community workers. The forum functions largely as a medium for communication and discussion, for example on special projects being run by individual churches, on funding, L.A. policy decisions affecting the area, such as policing, and runs a credit union. At the meeting attended by the researcher an approach for help with finding premises was made by two men in the process of establishing a work training scheme for people of Pakistani origin in the area. They had been brought by a community worker from a voluntary agency.

Method of Study

i) The information about the activities engaged in by the church and on the church premises noted above were collected from a variety of sources: the minister, the secretary to the Church Family Committee and the Property Steward, and the researcher's observations on attendance at several morning services (at which notices of the week's activities are given verbally) and some mid-week events.

ii) The means for finding out how individual members of this Christian community described and understood their relations to members of non-Christian religious communities was a questionnaire, a copy of which appears in Appendix A. This was personally administered by the researcher. Some factual information has been collected, namely sex, age group, occupation, residence, offices held in the church and extent of participation in church activities. In the second part of the questionnaire participants were asked about their contacts with people of other religions, their knowledge of their beliefs, their attitudes to them, their opinion on whether effort ought to be made to convert them, experiences at work and in the neighbourhood etc. The questionnaire was designed to provide a framework in which people could relate what was important to them. The researcher gave considerable freedom in allowing the participants to talk about matters which they felt to be relevant, although they did not appear to be directly answering the questions. This proved to be illuminating, particularly regarding the level of concern about the ecumenical dimensions of Christianity and the limited black/white integration in the church. In several instances, despite the terms of reference, 'other denominations' were referred to interchangeably with 'other religions' and the connection of 'other religions' with 'other colours' led to thinking about colour differences amongst Christians. These issues are dealt with under the heading "The Not-So-Hidden Agenda: Otherness". The interviews were carried out between 26th October and 21st November 1988, either on the church premises or in the homes of the participants.

The Participants

The researcher addressed the congregation during the morning service on 2nd October 1988, giving an introduction to her research into how Methodists relate to people of other faiths and inviting everybody to participate by answering some questions. Twenty people volunteered (out of a congregation of approximately 90). Two of these were subsequently eliminated as they were visiting theological students, and one of the twenty, having failed two appointments, was not followed up again. The invitation to participate was repeated at morning service two weeks later by the minister and other people presented themselves to the researcher during the following weeks. In total, 33 people took part in the survey: this represents approximately one third of an average morning congregation and one fifth of the official Church Membership.

Participants were therefore volunteers from the worshipping community. No effort was made to distinguish full Members of the Methodist Church from attenders. In the text "members" refers to those attending the church, whether full Members or not. As volunteers, the participants were self-selected. No statistical significance is therefore to be attached to the results of the questionnaire, but the sample, in fact, proved to be representative of a morning congregation in terms of age, sex, colour and occupational status. The representative validity of the sample was confirmed by the knowledge of the minister, and in relation to age, sex and colour, by the personal observation of the researcher. 20 participants were female (16 white, 4 black) and 13 male (8 white and 5 black). Table 1 illustrates the age distribution; black and white participants are shown individually because of the relationship found between age and colour involvement in 'outreach' activities noted above.

Table 1: Age Distribution of Participants

	White	Black	Total
14 - 18	1	0	1
19 - 25	1	1	2
26 - 35	0	0	0
36 - 45	4	0	4
46 - 55	1	4	5
56 - 65	6	3	9
66 - 75	5	1	6
76 & over	6	0	6

Thus more than one third (12 out of 33) of the sample are over 66 years of age and almost two thirds (22 out of 33) are over 56 years of age. The four age bands ranging from 14-45 have only 7 people between them, there being no participants in the 26-35 age group.

Table 2: Occupation of Participants

	Male	Female	Total
Paid employment	7	7*	14
Homemaker	0	4**	4
F/PT Further Ed.	0	3*	3
Retired	6	8	14

* 2 women were engaged in paid employment and further education, and have been counted twice. Hence the total of participants appears as 35.

** 2 of the Homemakers are of retirement age, but are included in this category as they were not previously engaged in paid employment.

All the participants fell within one of these categories. No-one was unemployed and looking for work.

Twenty-two of the 33 participants lived within one mile of the church and most of the rest within a mile and a half. Many had lived in the area all their lives and 23 participants had lived in the same house for more than 10 years, 17 of them for more than 20 years. Only one person out of the 33 had definite plans to leave the area (to move from a house to a bungalow), though a few said they would have liked to move had property values not fallen relative to other parts of the city. The picture presented is of a very settled and stable community.

The views of participants on Christian relations with people of other faiths cannot be assumed to be representative of this Methodist community, despite the age, sex and colour distribution of the sample being representative of the congregation as a whole (and certainly no claims are made that this particular church is representative of all Methodist churches in pluralist areas). Many factors could have influenced individuals' decisions not to participate: dislike of surveys; feeling they had no knowledge or experience to contribute on the subject; holding opinions which they felt were unacceptable (the minister has firm views and expresses them); or, as one woman was overheard to say, "talking about that sort of thing only leads to trouble". However, a range of views and experience were elicited, and the minister confirmed that the people who did participate would reflect the variety of attitudes held in, and in the proportions that would be representative of, the congregation. We now examine the responses to the interviews.

The Results of the Questionnaire

Contacts with People of Other Religions

Fourteen of the participants (8 female, 6 male) had neighbourly contacts with people of other religions which extended to visiting each others' houses. A further 8 engaged in conversation 'over the fence', 7 had no contact, and the remaining 4 had no nearby neighbours of other religions. One married couple and two ladies living alone mentioned that while they had accepted invitations to others' homes, neighbours of other faiths had not accepted invitations to come to their homes. Neighbourly contacts were defined by the participants in terms of looking after each others' houses when one was absent, taking in milk, exchanging cards and gifts (Christmas, births) and helping in emergencies. In a few cases the contact was almost daily. Many people described their relations with neighbours of other faiths as "friendly", though this covered superficial 'passing the time of day' to more practical, reciprocal neighbourliness.

Seven (out of 7) men and 4 (out of 7) women had contact at work and only one reported any personal difficulty arising from religion and this was a woman who felt under pressure from young male Muslims who appeared to resent her authority. The participant drew attention to the contribution of age, sex and colour factors in this situation. One man referred to tension between Hindu and Sikh workmates during the conflict at the Golden Temple in Amritsar. Five retired participants had also formerly worked alongside colleagues and with clients of other religions, also without problem. One person commented that work had been disrupted most by a Seventh Day Adventist who wanted time off to get to services. In a work situation people appeared simply to "get on with the job": as one woman put it, "you've got to get on, you can't work on your own." Another person commented that there was more potential tension at work with Jehovah's Witnesses because of the way they interpreted the Bible.

The three women engaged in further education all had friends of other religions from college, and one of them who had grown up in the area had had many friends at school (and learnt about other religions and completed a project on Sikhism). Several parents of young adult children mentioned that when their children were at school they had brought friends of other religions home and in one case the whole family had been invited to a Sikh wedding. One couple attended school and Scout functions (not the church Scouts) with families of other faiths. They were one of only two couples with school-age children.

Observations:
Work, education and close residential proximity were all productive of interaction between Christians and people of other faiths. Only one woman in the sample had had contact with people of other faiths through a church outreach activity (Brownies). The outreach activity which involved most people-power, the lunch club, involved no-one of other faiths. (It is important to note that the club catered for elderly people, so language was a very real barrier to involving people of other faiths in this age group.) No members of the church were involved with the ongoing work of the multi-faith and multi-cultural help centre run on the premises, though the researcher found a Sikh and a Hindu member of staff eager to talk about religion (forms of worship and experience) when she dropped in.

In the concluding chapter of Faith in the City of Birmingham, (the report of the Anglican Diocesan Commission examining the problems and opportunities in Birmingham's Urban Priority

Areas) the committee under the chairmanship of Lesslie Newbigin suggests as one of the four guiding principles for operating as 'a Community among other Communities' that:

> "the local congregation must be a place where people of all faiths can find a welcome. Formal inter-faith dialogue is an exercise for those with expert knowledge of the different faith-traditions, but we can all be involved in normal neighbourly conversation - and this should include all our neighbours and should provide the opportunities to learn of the religious experience of our neighbours, to share our faith and to communicate the invitation of a caring congregation."(1)

Two thirds of the participants were involved in "normal neighbourly conversation". But to say no more than this is to underestimate the practical caring, respect and mutual gratification which many of the participants demonstrated in their relations with people of other faiths and the actual living-out of accepting people for what they are as individuals, despite differences of religion and colour. Common humanity first, divisions second! There was no apparent relationship between the age, sex, or colour of the participants and the extent of contact with people of other faiths.

Knowledge of other Religious Beliefs

Twenty-two of the 33 participants said they had no knowledge of the beliefs of other religions; 17 of them were not interested in gaining such knowledge, 5 were. There was frequent confusion between Sikhism, Hinduism and Islam (e.g. "The Sikhs or Muslims regard the cow as holy"; "Sikhs pray to different gods for different things"). The other 11 who had some knowledge and were interested had varying amounts and sorts of knowledge gained from different sources - friends and neighbours, church discussion groups, an ecumenical meeting, books, media, and school.

The woman who appeared to have the most regular contact and intimate relationship with her Sikh neighbours was acutely discerning about differences (and changes) in cultural behaviour, practices and attitudes, and yet had no knowledge or interest in their religious beliefs. One man who described positive regular neighbourly and work contacts with Sikhs said he did not know about their beliefs but would like to, adding, "they seem a bit reserved about their religious beliefs." One man whose interest in religion was academic and professional took initiatives in visiting various places of worship and talking with people of other religions. Another man who described good working relationships with Muslims and was interested in knowing more about their religion had suggested reciprocal visits with them to mosque and church, but this had not been taken up.

Observations:

There is no clear connection between having knowledge of other religions, being interested in other religions and the nature of the relationship between individual Christians and people of other faiths. In only a few cases was knowledge and interest combined with strong neighbourly and working relationships.

Ought Christians Try to Convert People of Other Faiths?

This proved a difficult question for many participants, who were aware of a tension between the evangelistic dimension of Christianity and the way they related to people of other faiths, or, if they had little or no contact, what the nature of the relationship should be. Here are some of the 14 examples of 'ambivalence'.

> "That's a sticky one! I wouldn't go out of my way to say 'you must change'. You can do a lot by example."

> "No - unless they were involved with a religion of the sword. For example, if I met an Iranian-Ayatollah type of religion I would say it was cruel and not in the Koran, but if I talked to other people and thought they had loving God beliefs I wouldn't try to convert them to Christianity."

> "No - its not fair - and yet, it might be. If I can't get my husband to come, what right have I to push Muslims or whatever?"

> "This is a difficult question. I think I should find it very difficult and wonder if I was doing the right thing if they were sincere in their own beliefs. I don't know much about other religions ..... they may have many tenets Christians would agree with, but not, of course, in Jesus Christ as the Son of God."

> "No .....? Their culture is different to our culture, it would be wrong if they are happier and they help in society. I don't think we should force them. If they knew Christ ..... I would like them to know Christ. I think whoever comes to Christ is a different, happier person."

> "Its a bit hypocritical to say 'yes' but that's what I've always been told the Christian faith should do. But we've all got freedom of choice and if people want something they go looking for it. Should we offer it to people who don't want it? I wouldn't try and stop anybody."

> "Its complex. I'm inclined to think Jesus Christ is the one true way; we don't <u>know</u> there isn't any other way and that their religion is <u>not</u> as valid as our own."

Of the 3 people who felt that they ought to try and convert people of other faiths to Christianity, only one had contact with them. Fourteen of the participants felt that they ought not to try and convert - for a variety of reasons represented by the following responses.

> "Nobody should attempt to convert anybody to anything else. Missionary posture is wrong, discussion on one's faith and life-stance is right."
>
> "No. Because I don't think it's a thing a human being can do. Its something that comes from God."
>
> "I don't think I should put myself out to deliberately try and convert. If it came up and they wanted me to expound, yes. If they were interested I would be willing to do more."
>
> "I've never looked at it that way. From what they believe they seem to have the same interpretation as us in some respects. They seem to be more steadfast in their beliefs than us - I don't know why."
>
> "I wouldn't want anyone to convert my way of thinking. We are all entitled to our view of what God means to us personally."
>
> "I think they should be left to follow their own religion. They don't try to convert us, why should we try to convert them?"

Only 5 of the participants said that they had at one time or another talked about their own beliefs with people of other religions. Three of them had an 'ambivalent' attitude towards attempting to convert and the other two were definitely against trying to convert people of other faiths.

Observations:

Sensitivity to proselytising, it would appear, sprang largely from an ethical judgement - 'do as you would be done by' being the golden rule. Several people unsure of whether they should try to convert people pointed out that 'actions speak louder than words' and that living in a loving way was preferable to preaching:

> "Pushy evangelism, no. If you can't convert people by what you are, then there's no point ramming Christ down their throats!"

There was considerable resentment of the methods of the Jehovah's Witnesses' dogmatic and judgemental approach ("the man said I was a cannibal because I thought blood transfusions were alright"). One woman put criticism of this approach strongly:

> "The Islamic fundamentalists are like the moral majority in America. I hate fanatics; I can't cope with fanaticism - this urge to make everyone the same as you by whatever means. ..... There is a lack of respect, even contempt for other people: that's not part of Christianity and shouldn't be part of any other religion."

It was interesting that no-one expressed the fear that non-Christians were destined for hell. The saving of souls for the hereafter did not appear to be a major concern. The way of life here and now was the focus of attention and there was awareness of tension over 'mission' and of a lack of knowledge about other religions necessary to discriminate between beliefs before making any attempt to change people's religious adherence.

<u>What is held in common, if anything, between practising members of religions?</u>

Fourteen people felt they did have something in common with people of other faiths who took their religion seriously; 18 did not have any comment to make as they felt they did not have sufficient knowledge, and one was not a practising Christian.

Typical answers given by the 14 were:

> "We're all worshipping the same God".
>
> "The fact that we all have a God who we look to for guidance and help".
>
> "Most of them worship one God, so that's similar."
>
> "Its logic - if you believe there is only one God, if other people practise religions they must be worshipping the same God as you."

Two people identified "faith" rather than religion as being of prime importance in life:

> "Some people have no faith one way or the other: there's an old lady next door who has no faith and she is miserable. Some faith is the most important thing."
>
> "Faith keeps you going, some sort of faith. ..... In the end you are worshipping something that you can't see, that you just believe in. Eventually we are all worshipping the same person. Those who worship Buddha - he's just as real to them as Jesus is to us. Why knock them? Nobody knows."

One person commented that she had found that what she held in common with people of other faiths she had worked with was that they all desired to do good and as far as possible to get peace in the world.

Two people drew attention to the fact that most people's religion is determined by an accident of birth:

> "There is a common truth amongst all religious people, mainly in that they consider the common humanity of all peoples and that they are trying to live as good a life as possible by their lights as we are. Its only a question of geography which separates a lot of religions. In England fundamentally it's what family you were born in - you go to that persuasion."
>
> "We've got to respect everyone else's religion and teaching. Ours we learn from our ancestors: Chinese, Hindus - everyone worships in a different form. Our method is what we learn and we have to hold on to that."

The importance of parental practice for deciding religious affiliation was mentioned by three other participants in different contexts.

Observations:
The underlying assumption of those who felt religious people had something in common was that religion was about God and it therefore followed that people who practised a religion must be concerned with God. (Three people specifically pointed out that Buddhism could not be included on this count.) If this is taken together with the limited knowledge most people had about other religions, then religious pluralism is seen superficially as a diversification of theocentric worship patterns and ritual.

The Teaching of the Methodist Church on Christian Relations with People of Other Faiths

This question provoked one of three responses: a) people did not know what the official Methodist position was on relations with people of other faiths; b) they thought it was that Methodists should have respect and tolerance and agreed with this; or c) they thought the Methodist position was to have respect and tolerance and disagreed with this.

The largest group (20) did not know; 11 people thought the Church was in favour of an attitude of respect and tolerance towards people of other religions and agreed with this - 8 of them referred specifically to the teaching of the minister as the authority (only 2 participants out of the 33 had read any Methodist literature on other faiths). Two people who considered the Methodist Church taught respect and tolerance of other religions were highly critical of this stance:

> "Conference would like to lay down the law - most of it's rubbish..... altering lines of hymns! If they have a policy it is that we should go the way of the other religions. ..... We are supposed to go to their services. I don't want to, I'm happy with my own."

> "There isn't another religion that will hold things together like ours - it's for individuals, societies and the world. The Hindus and Sikhs are not settled. Jews are alright but they don't mix. Muslims try to take over with their religion. I read in the paper they are building one new mosque a week. We shan't be a Christian country soon. The fact we are willing to let that happen is an indictment."

Observations:

Finding that almost two thirds of participants were unaware of Methodist teaching on relations with people of other faiths is not surprising to the researcher: the fact that Methodism is a 'broad church' is noted in the section on Ecumenism below and the adoption of reports by Conference on various issues does not carry the weight of "official teaching", and to this extent the question was possibly misleading (thus engendering the shocked response of one person, "We can think what we like, can't we?"). That there is currently much discussion and disparate opinion within the bureaucratic structure of the Methodist Church and a lack of coherence in addressing the whole issue of interfaith dialogue will be seen in the following section. Those who discerned an attitude of respect and tolerance (the importance of the minister for influencing views is noted) are in tune with the fundamental starting point of WCC and BCC literature adopted by the Methodist Church and referred to in the Faith and Order Statements (Section 3).

<u>What Participants Considered to be God's Feelings about People of Other Religions</u>

The largest group of 19 people considered that God felt the same about all people:

> "He has the same love for everyone. We are all equal in his sights".
>
> "There are some people who think there will only be white Christians in heaven and they're going to be in for a shock."
>
> "If there is one God, as we Christians believe, then he must love all his children."
>
> "He made them all. It doesn't say in the Bible he made Christians in his own image. It says he made mankind in his own image."
>
> "I think he loves them just as much as he loves me."

Four additional participants were more specific in their comments; for example,

> "He's probably sad at the things we do - and in other religions - which are opposite to what he wants. ..... Whichever faith, there are people who don't show God's true love. They worship in a way. He does feel upset - that's on all faiths."
>
> "He is glad they believe, I should think; they believe in something and go for it."
>
> "If people are good and live a decent life and believe in what they believe, I think they are acceptable to God."

Seven people said they did not know how God felt and three of them were surprised at the question (e.g. "I haven't got a hot line to God!"). For one person, a humanist, the question was not applicable. Of the remaining two, one person replied that the worship of idols or images was not acceptable to God and the other referred to God's forgiving nature.

Observations:
It would appear that for the majority of Methodists interviewed in this study, relationships with people of other faiths are, as we concluded in the first chapter, "set firmly in humanity's relation to God as the Universal Creator and Sustainer."

The Not-So-Hidden Agenda: 'Otherness'

The Introduction to the questionnaire was read carefully to each participant:

> "The purpose of the study is to find out how members of a Christian community describe and understand their relation to members of non-Christian religious communities (Hindus, Buddhists, Sikhs, Jews, Muslims)."

After a few interviews, which revealed a marked tendency on the part of the respondents to talk about other Christian denominations, a further statement was added to reinforce the purpose:

> "so I am not concerned with Methodist relations with other Christian denominations, but with how Methodists relate to people of other religions."

None of the questions referred to ecumenical issues or colour, but these areas were introduced by respondents in relation to a variety of the questions. It is emphasized that these issues were not raised by the researcher: two observations must be made regarding this. Firstly, the material presented provides a limited picture in that all the participants did not address the subjects; secondly, the fact that the issues were put forward spontaneously and repeatedly indicates their importance to the respondents. What emerged from the attempt to identify Christian relations with people of other faiths may be described as the underlying issue of 'Otherness'.

The 'other' presented by participants, triggered by the questions on relations with other religions in this study, was other Christians - white, black and brown. We shall attend to the most prominent areas in which differentiation was experienced - a) other denominations and b) other colours: the notes in brackets following the quotations indicate Female/Male, White/Black, and the age group of the respondents.

a) Other denominations

A third of the respondents, quoted below, specifically related inter-faith to intra-faith issues in some way. It has been noted that this church is particularly committed to ecumenical involvement and it is clear that members of this congregation are aware of the processes of identifying differences and what is held in common between denominations. Positive and negative conclusions are drawn about the effects of diversity of belief. Through this, attention is directed to the perceived gap between belief and practice in Christianity. Eight respondents (black and white) spoke very critically, from personal experience, of the Jehovah's Witnesses judgemental and dogmatic attitude on doctrinal issues. (The question of the Christian nature of this sect is not entered into here.)

In reply to "Do you feel you ought to try and convert people of other religions?"

> "We are so fragmented in denominations. How do you explain to somebody that basically we all believe in the same things. Who are we to say ....? I always tried to point out we are a religion of love, but they say 'what's happening in Northern Ireland? Put your own house in order before anybody else's'." (F, W, 56-65)

> "That's difficult. I wouldn't want to push my opinions on anyone else." This was based on the experience (related in detail) of denominational tensions in the family raised by a Methodist/Roman Catholic marriage. (F, W 66-75)

In reply to "Is there anything we have not talked about that you think is important in Christian relations with people of other religions?"

> "I think combined services with other Christian denominations is important because it is showing others that Christians are trying not to be divided. ..... It's like strands of rope being twisted together: single strands break easily." (F, W, 56-65)

> "Religion has caused more wars than anything - look at Northern Ireland." (F, W, 56-65)

> "I don't like Methodist, Roman Catholic, whatever. We are all walking down the same road hoping to find the same God. Jehovah's Witnesses - I wouldn't call that a religion. The Pentecostals have the attitude that they are the only Christians." (M, B, 56-65)

> "I think the various churches and different religions should work together to do things in community relations and not make a 'them and us' situation. Just like we have inter-church things (in some areas there is cut-throat competition!) we should work with different faiths. We all have one thing in common which is to work out the best way to live." (F, W, 14-18)

> "Grass roots people forced more inter-denominational events and get-togethers. ..... It is really good experience, sharing beliefs and explanations. Now we're just Christians." (F, W, 35-45)

In reply to "What do you think the official Methodist Church teaching is about how Christians should behave in relation to people of other religions" and "What is your feeling about this?"

> "Don't set out to convert them and don't set out to ignore them. You're never going to get that far: we have enough trouble trying to get our people to work alongside people of other denominations. ..... Christians have learnt through ecumenism that each denomination is not the only right one - we have learnt through that in our attitudes to other religions. ..... We ought to get relations and recognition amongst brothers and sisters in Christ first, before we turn to other religions." (M, W, 35-45)

In reply to "Do you feel you would like them (people of other religions) better if they were Christians?"

> "I accept people at face value. There are differences between Christian denominations: in my (extended) family there are people very committed to their own denominations who don't have anything to do with each other, so it doesn't matter if people are of other religions - they speak to me and I speak to them. Religious beliefs don't matter. A person can be a good person without <u>any</u> religious beliefs. There are chaps at work who never darken the door of a church but who do a lot of good work." (M, W, 35-45)

In reply to "How do you think God feels about the people of other religions?"

> "That's difficult. I wouldn't know to be honest. The people that go to the Church of God (black-led Pentecostal) think they are right and that others are not Christian because they have not been baptised. (2) We are not highly emotional like the Pentecostals: they shout and are too emotional. They think they are right." (F, B, 46-55)

> "I don't think religion is that important: it is the way you think in yourself. Hindu, Sikh, Muslim, Methodist - may have your religions but that is not important. What is important is the kind of life you live, having a clean hand and a pure heart. The pure in heart shall see God. I could be a good Roman Catholic and deep down still doing wrong. If you haven't got love, in spite of your religion, its not that important." (M, B, 46-55)

b) Other colours

Tom Driver points out that 'otherness' is an ethical question, and therefore also a theological one.(3) Rosemary Ruether discusses the 'otherness' of women in Christianity, which is dominated by male images and has been documented and formulated by men in such a way as to push women to the fringes of religious life. She notes a parallel between the condescension shown to women and the condescension shown to other religions by Christianity.(4) That people of religions other than Christianity in Britain are, more often than not, (though not exclusively) of another colour and culture presents an intricate complex of factors which, it is probably fair to say, is similarly currently recognised, but not fully understood. The history of Methodist overseas mission discussed in the next chapter explains in some measure the attitudes inherent in the Methodist tradition to these factors. White people within the church who feel that the influx of coloured immigrants has been detrimental to the well-being of white Britains (5 participants referred to the lowering in value of houses as a result of coloured immigrants in the area) are not likely to be well inclined or well placed to share religious experiences and beliefs with Muslims, Sikhs or Hindus, particularly when they are barely on speaking terms with fellow Christians in the same congregation who are black.(5)

The researcher commends three works produced from very different perspectives which contribute some insight into the issues and underline the complexities: the major Methodist report A Tree God Planted: Black People in British Methodism (1985); Dervla Murphy, Tales From Two Cities (1987), which contains a personal account of her experience and observations in a pluralist area of Birmingham; and Colonial Immigrants in a British City: A class analysis (1979), by John Rex and Sally Long, which reports on a study in Birmingham. For our present purposes, it is deemed most appropriate to record the comments made by the respondents and let them speak for themselves.

'The Indian Christians'

The Indian Christians are a distinct group of mainly first generation Punjabi/English speaking Christians converted in

India. They attached themselves to the church, having had to leave rented premises after some disorder. Although they moved to their own place of worship a year ago they still keep the connection with the church. According to the minister this is because they wish to retain a denominational allegiance and because they are not registered for weddings. Joint services are held once every two months at alternate locations and supported by 15-20 church members. Five respondents mentioned that they attended these services. The minister is keen to maintain the connection, though finds meaningful communication difficult with this "fundamentalist" and "anti-Sikh" group. The researcher found that when respondents (black and white) mentioned the Indian Christians it was in quite a positive way, showing interest and a willingness to extend the hand of friendship - and accept the present situation. 'Otherness' was clearly recognised by the church and the Indian group, and confirmed by separation. As one respondent commented:

> "Did you know about the minister's attempts to involve the Punjabi Christians? An attempt at integration. If there is a difference there between Punjabi Christians and Methodist Christians, what chance for the rest? They felt they had to find their own premises in the end. The gap is getting larger - only a few go from the church." (M, W, 36-45)

And another:

> "We are trying very hard to fit them in. I have been down to their new premises - they did have part of ours. They are so pleasant, you know. The Indian Christians have the best of both worlds." (F, W, 76+)

Black and White

> "If only some of the white Christians would remember that the Lord is the Lord of the World. I am very troubled. Other Christian people around me are very down on them." (F, W, 76+)

"The black people tend not to get involved in weekday activities - I think it is because of their jobs and families." (F, W, 36-45)

"People smile at you in church and ignore you in the street. They don't want to talk to you. We need more unity and socialising with the members. If we are practising Christians we should be more sincere in these fields. You don't know whether you are free to go to meetings or socials - you don't know what sort of atmosphere you would come across. You come across these things outside, but you really <u>feel</u> it inside church." (F, B, 56-65)

"The minister tries to the utmost to combine people to accept each other in the church ..... There is the Indian Christians meeting and a black church meets there. Occasionally we have a black preacher. And it's catching on - people are turning up." (M, B, 46-55)

"If everybody tried really hard (a good many do) not only to shake hands but take an interest in folk. Some of them come to Women's Fellowship but they do not join in or say anything in the discussions. I was leaving at the same time as two of them one week and asked if they had enjoyed it. They said, 'Mm, but we didn't have anything from the Book'. <u>We</u> like things like cookery talks and talks about people's interesting holidays. They will like it this afternoon because X is speaking and there will be a (Bible) theme." (F, W, 76+)

"Its important coloured people shouldn't be thrust down our throats and vice-versa. Our minister is always saying we must make a fuss and give them office and so on. I think we should be left to find our level. Its no good saying we're the same. We have common meeting grounds, get on, why push for everything to be the same?" (F, W, 76+)

"There are things you'd like to define. When blacks came into this country, the spirit of the people here - at home we thought, a loving people - was not what we came to find ...... Scripture says love and respect every nation. Because of our colour we weren't wanted - our skin, not our ways - prejudice. Is this really Christianity?" (M, B, 66-75)

Summary of Findings

Interfaith dialogue and encounter is not viewed as a major priority for this church. Mission does not appear to be a focus of activity, either towards people of other faiths or none and most available energy is geared, as it probably is in most Methodist churches with large premises to keep and an established fabric of meetings, to the maintenance of corporate fellowship.[6] That issues of ecumenism and colour loom large in the consciousness of the participants when asked to consider people of other faiths is indicative of the attention which needs to be paid to these areas in the Methodist tradition.

In that only a minority of participants had no contact with people of other faiths, and that all those who did have contact welcomed it, there is a foundation for interfaith dialogue. It is not yet taking place, either as a church-based venture, or by individual members of the congregation, with the exception of two or three people. Lack of knowledge about other religions, their beliefs and modes of worship contribute to this situation: whereas the findings showed that the establishment of relationships with people of other faiths did not depend on the knowledge possessed about the faiths, it is possible that it does limit the development of those relationships into ones of mutual understanding and sharing of beliefs and experience.

The area on which there seemed to be most agreement was the Universal Lordship of God and the implication this carried for relationships with people of other faiths, in that they were perceived as being, like them, children of God. Combined with overall disinclination to judge other religions (the few exceptions were, however, strongly critical), even when people were firm in their conviction that Christianity was the best religion, or to consider members of other faiths excluded from the possibility of heaven, would suggest a theocentric orientation to the theology of interfaith dialogue. However, the tensions evident in the responses to the question on conversion indicate the difficulty many people have in reconciling commitment to Christianity with an attitude of tolerance and acceptance towards other religions. That this is a difficulty shared by the Methodist establishment and theologians was unrecognised by participants; few people seemed to have shared it with each other, either.

Most participants held, explicitly or implicitly, that God created everyone, loved everyone and would judge everyone according to "their own lights". With this, as we shall see below, they would find John Wesley in agreement. He would no doubt also commend efforts to 'love your neighbour'. Whether Wesley has anything further to teach Methodists in pluralist societies on interfaith dialogue and encounter we shall explore in Chapter IV. Meanwhile we continue our research into contemporary Methodism and other faiths by examining the way in which the institutional church is approaching it.

2. Divisions of Responsibility: Church Organisation

The annual Conference is the ultimate authority of the Methodist Church, subject to the governing legislation, the Principal Act being the Methodist Church Act of 1976.(7) Items of the agenda are adopted or rejected by democratic vote of the 576 lay and ordained representatives. John Wesley, in contrast, had been "Methodism's executive, legislative and judiciary combined"; he summoned his preachers to conference for them to advise, not govern, and controlled where and how his ministers were to work.(8) The location of power after his death was a major source of continuing contention for many decades, along with the relation of Methodism to the Church of England (see Chapter III.2). Robert Currie sees a connection between Wesley's authoritarianism and his emphasis on Christian Perfection to have been influential in organisational change:

> "The ideal of religious democracy emerged in the conflict between the interests of local communities created almost incidentally in the search for perfection, and the demands of a disciplinarian hierarchy. This ideal required a religion of liberty, community and personal responsibility". (9)

Some Methodists during Wesley's lifetime struggled against his personal control of the connexion and various factions after his death (he had appointed the Legal Hundred to constitute the Conference by Deed of Settlement in 1784) struggled to win lay representation and democratic decision making. Both these battles have been long won, but the organisation is not without its contemporary critics. David Clark in his booklet What Future for Methodism? suggests that the present system is "captive" to bureaucracy, (together with clericalism, parochialism and denominationalism) which is designed to maintain the system at the expense of freedom to respond to the movement of the Spirit:

> "We are pre-occupied with imprisoning agencies from church council to Conference and hidebound by having every detail of our corporate life mapped out for us. Tedious duplications and repetition abound as we seek to pass a mountain of data up and down through every tier of a very hierarchical structure." (10)

The Structure of The Methodist Church*

CONFERENCE

Held annually
576 representatives: equal lay & ordained
Annually elected President and Vice President
Permanent Secretary to Conference

PRESIDENTS COUNCIL

CONNEXIONAL COMMITTEES
General Purposes
Faith & Order
Law & Polity
Stationing
Methodist Publishing House & Epworth Press
Ecumenical
Sub-com. Local Ecumenical Development

Secs. appointed by Conference

THE DIVISIONS
Home Mission
Overseas Missions
Ministries
Education & Youth
Social Responsibility
Finance
Property

Secs. appointed by Conference

DISTRICTS
Chairmen
District Synods
Committees:
District Policy
Home & Overseas Missions
Education & Youth and Social Responsibility
Ministries
Property

CIRCUITS
Superintendent Ministers
Committees:
General Purposes
Home & Overseas Missions
Education & Youth
Property
Women
Social Responsibility

LOCAL CHURCHES
Circuit Ministers
Church Councils
General Church Meetings

* Information collated from The Constitutional Practice and Discipline of the Methodist Church, Volume 2, 1988.

The ideal of a religion of "liberty, community and personal responsibility" would now seem to be in conflict with a bureaucratic hierarchy.

It is not our purpose here to discuss the organisational strengths and shortcomings of the Methodist Church, but simply to observe the outline of policy making structures and the committee system which dominates all levels of decision-making, in order to understand the manner in which the question of Methodist relations with people of other faiths moves within the system. The full-time professional administrators, the Secretaries of the Connexional Committees and the Divisions, together with the Presidents Council (composed of the Secretaries of the Divisions, 6 Chairmen of Districts, 2 Circuit Ministers, 6 lay representatives, 4 others appointed annually and the Chairman of the Budget Committee) form a focal triangle of executive influence directed by and reporting to the annually convened one-week Conference (see Chart, page 62). Reports adopted by Conference together with the Statements of the Methodist Church on Faith and Order represent the policy of the Methodist Church in Britain.

Interfaith dialogue and encounter emerges as an issue in the work of the various Divisions and Connexional Committees; responsibilities are divided, as are ways of approaching and dealing with questions which arise within their spheres of activity - whether these are matters of Law and Polity affecting the use of premises, or the theological basis of evangelism in a pluralist society.

The Faith and Order Committee was given the task in 1983 of examining how Methodism should relate to people of other religions. The Methodist Overseas Division is having to face the implications for mission of the recognition of pluralism (see p.86). The Home Mission Division has responsibility for the new full time appointment of a minister, Martin Forward, to work in this area and for the Committee on Relations with People of Other Faiths, which is inter-divisional in its composition, of which the appointed minister is secretary. This committee was formed to facilitate and encourage 'local dialogue', monitor 'the experience of groups coping with problems at the practical level' and prepare an 'Interfaith Resource Pack'.

Donald English, (General Secretary of the Home Mission Division), in his booklet Evangelism Now, which is based on a report presented to and accepted by Conference in 1986, points out that the Division was given the responsibility of relations with people of other faiths "in order to preserve the evangelistic dimension".(11) In this 30-page publication the 13 lines devoted to "Relations with Other Faiths" are mostly concerned with principles of dialogue - respect of the other person's view, effort to understand them and to be willing to learn as well as to teach, while remaining "firm in the desire to commend Jesus Christ as Saviour and Lord". Donald English feels lessons could be learned from this "sharp definition" of dialogue and evangelism for all areas of evangelism and concludes by commenting that most Christians in Britain have little experience in inter-faith dialogue.

The 1988 Home Mission Resource Catalogue contains no material on other world religions or interfaith dialogue. The 1987 Annual Review presented no articles on multi-faith issues; the 1986 Review contained one short article by a "community pastor" who started a group for Muslims and Christians. He was employed with a grant from the Multi Racial Projects Fund, which is supported by Home Mission, the Overseas Division and the Division of Social Responsibility.(12)

It is the Division of Social Responsibility (DSR) which at present offers most guidance on "Multi Faith Society", listing 2 booklets and 2 pamphlets on relations with people of other faiths and 1 pamphlet each on Islam and Sikhism; the remaining two publications in the "Multi Faith Society" section are "The Agony of Ireland" and "The H-Bloc Issue"! DSR also produced a booklet in the late 1970s entitled Shall we greet only our own family?, which explores the possibilities and difficulties of dialogue and suggests ways for Christians to prepare themselves for relations with people of other faiths. This Division is concerned with race and community relations, international relief and development, 'social' issues (e.g. housing, drugs, poverty), human rights etc. As a Circuit DSR secretary commented, "they have made relations with people of other religions a Problem".

The Home Mission Division and the Faith and Order Committee (taking account of the work done by the Division of Ministries) reported to Conference in 1985 and 1986 respectively on "Sharing in God's Mission"(13) and "The Ministry of the

People of God".[14] On the first page of each report acknowledgement is made of the presence of pluralist societies in Britain and the need to re-assess mission. The Home Mission committee admits to being:

> "far from monochrome in its views, but is determined to face together questions raised by our Multi-Faith Society; such as 'Can we learn about God from people of other Faiths? How are we to expound the uniqueness of Christ in a Multi-Faith society? How is the Spirit of God at work among non-Christians? We face such questions ..... 'as Christians who love the Lord Jesus and who believe him to be Lord of all'." (15)

The Division of Education and Youth also shares a concern for Methodist relations with people of other faiths. The recently appointed General Secretary, the Reverend C. Hughes Smith, was asked to comment on the Education Reform Act; part of his reply says:

> "I believe we must also recognise that part of the Christianity represented in our tradition of Arminianism is to underwrite and fund the multi-faith aspect of our community." (16)

Believing that the Methodist Church had been at the forefront in formulating "the mode of being a Christian in a multi-faith society", he emphasized in the same interview that:

> "minorities must not be treated in a cavalier fashion and toleration must be the watchword in a society that is becoming increasingly intolerant."

It is apparent that all seven Divisions of the Methodist Church (we assume that Finance and Property are by their nature involved in all aspects of institutional church life) are acutely aware of operating in a religiously plural society. The implications for mission and service are recognised, and the dilemmas and anxieties voiced. It is also clear that interfaith encounter and dialogue cannot be neatly boxed into its own pigeonhole, a subject of interest for a few enthusiasts: it raises questions affecting fundamental understanding of the Church's role and function - its mission.

Piecemeal, overlapping and diverse responses have been the outcome: the Home Mission Division has the responsibility for the Committee on Relations with People of Other Faiths, while the DSR has adopted the task of providing literature and sources of information on the subject, and is also much concerned with racism, an important aspect of relations with people of other faiths, as we noted in the church study.

3. Faith and Order Statements on Other Faiths

Three areas of The Methodist Church's concern are dealt with by the Faith and Order Statements: the Use of Trust Premises, Inter-faith Marriages and Relations with People of Other Faiths. The recommendations in the Statements of the Methodist Church on Faith and Order 1933-1983 are those accepted by Conference in the year presented. The first two reports adopted by Conference are dated 1972, and the third 1983. It would appear that practical, grass roots situations at local level produced the initial stimulus for theological and institutional reflection on the underlying implications of specific developments and brought these to the wider attention of Methodism.

(i) Use of Trust Premises

The Committee faced the dilemma of minority religious groups needing accommodation:

> "As human beings they have a right to freedom of worship, and Christians should help them to exercise their rights. Must this stop short of permitting worship in Methodist premises?" (17)

The bulk of the report consists of a summary of the committee's discussion, which outlines the diversity of views amongst Christians about other religions: some see continuity between the various faiths and find biblical evidence for knowledge and service of God outside the Jewish/Christian tradition, and some would feel that "Christ is present 'incognito' in other faiths". Others stress the discontinuity between "that to which Christians bear witness and all human forms of religion; God has said something in Christ which is a judgement on all religion". These Christians are concerned about the justification of continuing missionary work abroad if moves at home assume no proselytisation. "A group of immigrant Christians, admittedly fairly conservative in its outlook, has indeed expressed its disapproval." A third group of Christians, whilst holding the latter position felt that nevertheless, Christian charity should prevail.[18]

Two recommendations accepted by Conference were concerned specifically with the use of Methodist Premises: members of other faiths should be allowed to use them for "secular and social activities" and these could legitimately include an "incidental religious rite" such as saying grace at a meal, a blessing at a wedding reception, (the ceremony having taken place elsewhere), or an act of individual prayer demanded at a particular time. The other two recommendations were that local churches should take the initiative to establish dialogue with representatives of other faiths and that individual Christians should take opportunities for the "sympathetic observation" of other faiths and should "gladly accept whatever experience and communion with God arises in such relationships". This is followed by a warning that Christians should "scrupulously avoid those forms of interfaith worship which compromises the distinctive faiths of the participants and should ensure that Christian witness is neither distorted nor muted".(19) The distinctiveness of Christianity is to be preserved against "tendency to syncretism". (A working definition of syncretism given in the statement adopted by the WCC Theological Consultation on Dialogue in Community held at Chiang Mai in 1977 reads "conscious or unconscious human attempts to create a new religion composed of elements taken from different religions".)(20)

The majority of the committee took the view that in certain circumstances (when no other building was available, on a temporary basis, subject to the satisfaction of the superintendent and congregation "that the worship will not either in word or act be offensive to the Christian conscience"), it should be made permissible for premises to be used for worship by other faiths. This recommendation was not accepted by Conference. If it had been, an act of parliament would have been necessary to change the provisions of the Model Deed. Conference apparently felt that more consideration needed to be given to the whole issue.

(ii) Inter-faith Marriages[21]

Pastoral counselling is given priority: the minister should discuss with the parties the religious, domestic and social implications of a marriage between a Christian and a member of another religion and "normal practice" should be to supplement a Registry Office ceremony with prayers in the home. If a marriage ceremony takes place in church, four conditions are suggested: the non-Christian partner respects the convictions, right to practice and right to bring up children in the Christian faith of the Christian partner; the non-Christian partner, having read the service, should be willing to take part in it; nothing should be added to the structure of the service; and the omissions should be minimal.

How these statements are interpreted and implemented in the various and complex situations presented to the ordained ministry at the cutting edge would require a study in itself. Martin Forward in an article entitled "The Pastor's Opportunities", which appeared in The Expository Times,[22] gives some examples of decisions he has had to make as a Methodist Minister in Leicester.

(iii) Relations With People of Other Faiths[23]

> "We understand dialogue to be a proper part of the total mission we are called to - a mission which is rooted in the belief that God, as Jesus Christ has revealed him, is not simply the God of Christians but the God of the whole universe."

Methodist concern for working ecumenically is particularly evident in multi-faith matters. The committee's statement under this heading immediately draws attention to the British

Council of Churches booklet Relations with People of Other Faiths: Guidelines on Dialogue in Britain (1981) and commends it to the study of the Methodist people.

The General Synod of the Church of England also considered the BCC booklet in 1981 and accepted the principles of dialogue. Its Board for Mission and Unity was asked to prepare a report on the theological aspects of dialogue. Towards a Theology for Inter-Faith Dialogue was published in 1984 and stresses the need to work with other ecumenical partners through the BCC's Committee for Relations with People of Other Faiths. Kenneth Cracknell (as Secretary of the BCC committee) was a member of the group which prepared the Report.

Forging the Methodist link, the Faith and Order statements then refer to supporting views to be found in John Wesley's Sermon XCI "On Charity" (referring to Romans 10:12):

> "He 'is rich in mercy' to all who call upon him according to the light they have, and 'in every nation, he that feareth God and worketh righteousness is accepted of him'".

Drawing again on the BCC booklet, the Committee examine what dialogue involves: entering conversations, listening in love, mutual respect, openness to seeing what God has done in other traditions, recognising that the truth is greater than anyone has grasped, being part of a community and co-operation on justice and peace issues. It then emphasizes that none of these things inhibits the Christian:

> "from witnessing to his experience of the universal Lordship of Christ in the presence of people of other faiths, though it will affect the manner in which it is done." (24)

On proselytising, the statement reads:

> "Christians involved in formal interfaith meetings will refrain from using these opportunities for soliciting converts. The Church's ministry of preaching for decision will be exercised on other more appropriate occasions. Nevertheless such preaching and evangelism ought always to be sensitive to the principles of dialogue." (25)

Methodism affirms the four principles of dialogue (in line with WCC and BCC): dialogue begins when people meet each other; dialogue depends on mutual understanding and mutual trust; dialogue makes it possible to share in service to the community; and dialogue becomes the medium of authentic witness.

4. Summary

Interfaith encounter and dialogue is not an irrelevance for Methodists; it would, however, appear to be a problem for many.

Among the Methodist community in a religiously plural area of Birmingham surveyed many people do consciously make the effort to 'love their neighbours' and have established relationships with people of other faiths with whom they work, study and share the neighbourhood. Very few engage in mutual communication about religious beliefs, practices or experiences or wish to do so. Most would base this on an attitude of respect and tolerance deriving from God's love for all humanity, which as a starting point is very positive. Where to go and how to get there remain unanswered questions - if indeed they are raised at all.

We have seen in our brief examination of the Divisions and Connexional committies of the Methodist Church that questions about relations with people of other faiths are being raised in all areas of the church's functioning - Home and Overseas Mission, Education, Social Responsibility, Property, Finance and Ministries. To a great extent the stimulus for articulating and addressing the issues has come from the need to deal with practical grass-roots situations. The theological implications become clear: if the presence of God is recognized in people of other religions should the Church be proselytising amongst them? If not, what is the nature of the Church's mission? Do Christians have anything to learn about the Kingdom of God from non-Christians if its boundaries are not confined to the Church?

What is also clear is the diversity of response within Methodism. This is reflected in the Faith and Order Statements on "Other Faiths". Rather than being a statement on how Methodists <u>should</u> view other religions, it is an attempt to indicate the variety of ways in which Methodist Christians <u>do</u> see Christianity in relation to other faiths, to define when it is appropriate to "preach for decision", and to open discussion on the role of dialogue in mission. The Statement is brief and unsystematic, reflecting the confusion over how to address the whole subject. The group established in 1983 to report to the Faith and Order Committee on relations with people of other faiths has, at the time of writing, yet to publish its findings.

It becomes necessary at this point to gain some understanding of the 'ethos' of Methodism and what it contributes to the present situation of uncertainty and diverse responses among Methodists. A realistic awareness of the formative and developing elements of the Methodist tradition will, it is hoped, not only illuminate the causes of some of the present difficulties, but also indicate directions in which change may be anticipated.

-oOo-

References

(1) Faith in the City of Birmingham: an examination of problems and opportunities facing a city, the Report of a Commission set up by the Bishop's Council of the Diocese of Birmingham, Chairman Sir Richard O'Brien, p.124.

(2) The 'baptism' referred to here in the black Pentecostal church is "Spirit baptism", the receiving of the gifts of the Holy Spirit, particulary glossolalia. Reference: Ian MacRobert, "The Function of Pneumatology in Black Churches", Lecture at Selly Oak Colleges, 31.1.89.

(3) Tom Driver, "The Case for Pluralism" in The Myth of Christian Uniqueness, eds. John Hick and Paul Knitter, p.209.

(4) Rosemary Ruether, "Feminism and Jewish-Christian Dialogue", Ibid, pp.137-148.

(5) In Colonial Immigrants in a British City, which reports on a study of class analysis in 4 Birmingham wards, John Rex and Sally Long found support for their thesis that the deterioration which white residents perceived, "was not an accelerated physical deterioration due to the misuse of buildings by black immigrants, but simply a deterioration of the area due to the fact that there were what were thought of as inferior, black, colonial men living there." P.92.

(6) Robert Currie draws attention to these factors in the first century of Methodism in Chapter 2 "Chapel Community and Denominational Conflict", Methodism Divided. (Denomination here refers to the variety of Methodist denominations which evolved.)

(7) The Constitutional Practice and Discipline of the Methodist Church Volume 1, p.3.

(8) Robert Currie, Methodism Divided: A Study in the Sociology of Ecumenism, p.22.

(9) Ibid, p.81.

(10) David Clark, What Future for Methodism?, pp.7-8.

(11) Donald English, Evangelism Now, pp.23-24.

(12) In an article by William Booker, Home Mission Annual Review 1986, pp.46-7.

(13) Home Mission Department of the Methodist Church, Sharing in God's Mission, the report approved by the 1985 Conference.

(14) Faith and Order Committee report The Ministry of the People of God, approved by the 1986 Conference.

(15) Home Mission Division, Conference Agenda 1985, pp.1-2.

(16) Avril Bottoms, "Integration of church young people urged", Methodist Recorder, November 10, 1988.

(17) Statements of the Methodist Church on Faith and Order 1933-1983, p.256.

(18) Ibid, pp.256-257.

(19) Ibid, p.258.

(20) Stanley Samartha, Editor, Faith in the Midst of Faiths, p.148.

(21) Statements of the Methodist Church on Faith and Order 1933-1983, p.259.

(22) Martin Forward "The Pastor's Opportunities" in The Expository Times Volume 99/6, March 1988.

(23) Statements of the Methodist Church on Faith and Order 1933-1983, pp.260-261.

(24) Ibid, p.261.

(25) Ibid.

CHAPTER III

THREE ELEMENTS OF METHODISM

Overseas Mission, Ecumenism and Christian Perfection

In this chapter we explore three formative and changing elements of Methodism which are relevant to the way it relates to the contemporary realities of Christianity as one of the world religions in a pluralist society.

A history of two and a half centuries of Methodism from the 'Holy Club' at Oxford to the present day is beyond the scope of the present work: the completed publication in 1988 of four volumes of such a record, the most recent amongst many, underlines the size and breadth of that task. A History of the Methodist Church in Great Britain has been used as the major reference source. Three aspects of Methodism - Overseas Mission, Ecumenism and Christian Perfection - have been selected as being particularly central to an understanding of the ethos of Methodism, and consequently to its relations with people of other faiths. Within each of these three sections the process followed is: i) examination of the origins; ii) review of particular historical situations to highlight major trends; and iii) identification of contemporary patterns and changing attitudes.

It is hoped that in the following, necessarily selective, appraisal, some insight will be gained into what Methodism brings to inter-faith dialogue and encounter.

1. Overseas Mission

The Methodist call "who is willing to go?" was not made in the first instance as a response to the need for the 'heathen' to be converted but to serve the needs of expatriate communities.

> "Soldiers, sailors, ships carpenters, traders: these were the sort of men who established the first Methodist societies in other countries, led class meetings and preached the Word. The Conference did not usually seem to be aware of what such pioneers were doing." (1)

Individuals like Nathaniel Gilbert in Antigua who called together his slaves and invited them into his home to tell them what Christ had done for him (1760),(2) pre-empted the launching of the Methodist Missionary Society and the Conference decision of 1786 to take responsibility for overseas missions. The Anglican revivalist movement developed in the throes of the Industrial Revolution and spread during the major period of colonial expansion, supported by:

> "a widely accepted theology which took seriously not only the place of Christians in the world but also man's desperate state in the light of eternity." (3)

The pattern of missionary work to non-Christians emanating from the needs of Britains resident in other countries was repeated; for example in 1811 the first Methodist missionary was sent to Africa, to Sierra Leone, together with three teachers, to minister to an established settlement, and in 1816 the English around Madras meeting for prayer and fellowship requested support.

> "Time after time, it was laymen emigrating or serving abroad who began a movement which soon developed to the point where it needed the full-time care of a trained minister.(4)

By 1932 there were 62 male and 35 female missionaries in West

Africa, who, together with 91 African ministers, served 70,000 full members and a total baptized community of 212,000. In South India there were 79 male and 78 female missionaries, 57 Indian ministers, 21,800 full members and a baptized community of 132,000.[5] (The membership figures of the Methodist Church in Britain in 1931 stood at 841,284.)[6]

N. Allen Birtwhistle, in his survey of Methodist Missions strongly disputes accusations that the early missionaries were "handmaids of white imperialism" and claims that this view is "as irrelevant and distorted as the myth that all colonial authority was devoted to unrelieved exploitation."[7] An article appearing in a Methodist Magazine of 1800 (apparently written by Thomas Coke), entitled 'A Short Account of the Success of the Methodist Missionaries in the West Indies' boasted of 11,000 conversions in the West Indies and stated of the converts: "their own masters confess that they are the best and most faithfull servants which they possess."[8] Evangelisation in such situations contributed to the maintenance and efficiency of the existing political and economic system for the benefit of the white 'masters', despite opposition to slavery and the slave trade by some Christians.[9] Earl Grey's statement of 1853 that the British crown "assists in diffusing amongst millions of the human race, the blessings of Christianity and civilization" was typical of the attitude of the time.[10] Accounts such as the one referred to above make explicit the emphasis on inculcating an awareness of personal sin and the search for individual salvation in the non-Christian population. This orientation combined with the interrelation of missionary enterprises and white colonialism clearly give some foundation to the accusations which Braithwaite disputes, of which, in retrospect, there can be no defence beyond the acknowledgement of the outstanding contributions made by many individual men and women to the quality of life of those they served.

However well intentioned, self-sacrificing (many died from tropical diseases, particularly in West Africa), and committed to improving the lot of the people they ministered to, it cannot but be acknowledged that the Methodist missionaries of the nineteenth century were part of the imperialist colonial scene, ministering initially to those continuing a British cultural and religious way of life in an alien environment which was regarded as lying in 'darkness'. Hymns from the nineteenth century such as "From Greenland's icy mountains" (801 The Methodist Hymnbook of 1933) popularised the idea that "they call us to deliver their land from errors chain./Can we, whose souls are lighted with wisdom from on high,/Can we to men benighted the lamp of life deny?" Emotive verses like "Little lips that Thou hast made/'Neath the far-off temples' shade/Give to gods of wood and stone/Praise that should be all thine own" (797 The Methodist Hymnbook) fuelled the enthusiasm at home, and the stirring chords of "Hills of the North rejoice" declared "though absent long, your Lord is nigh; He judgement brings and victory" (815, The Methodist Hymnbook). Kenneth Cracknell comments:

> "In this way the firm impression has been implanted cumulatively in the western Christian consciousness that God is absent from his world until the missionary comes with the message of Christ" (11)

The 'feedback' of the missionaries to the Methodist societies in Britain had apparently generally given a negative view of 'heathenism', with its idolatry and superstition, reports of cannibalism in Fiji, suttee and caste in India and foot-binding in China.(12) As Cracknell points out:

> "we can discern in their writing, in their letters home, and their public speaking when they were on leave, a tendency to see everything overseas in terms of spiritual darkness. They were, so to speak, programmed to see the darkest and basest side of the religions and cultures among which they ministered." (13)

In A History of Christian Missions, Stephen Neill provides a useful summary of missionary involvement in the South Pacific.(14) Drawing attention to the "ignorance, fear, and hatred, and a cruelty which regularly reached almost maniacal depths of bestiality" amongst the islanders, Neill reports the fateful outcomes of early enterprises at the end of the eighteenth century, when cannibalism was common. Methodism arrived some 20-30 years later and after patient groundwork, rapid progress was made following the conversion of the local chiefs. Neill refers to Professor Latourette's "acute" remarks on the spread of Christianity in Fiji relevant to almost all the islands:

> "The victory of Christians in warfare furthered the change of faith, for by the test of combat the Christian God had been proved more powerful than the old deities. Indeed on at least one occasion victorious Christians gave the vanquished pagans the choice of death or conversion." (15)

Presumably Christians killed in a gentlemanly fashion! There is no suggestion in Birtwhistle's references to Methodist missionary work in Fiji that the power of physical violence was utilized rather than the power of the word.

An interesting perspective on missionary work in the South Pacific is given by Sylvia Townsend Warner in her novel Mr. Fortune's Maggot, written in 1925. She relates the following conversation between two clergymen in the Islands in 1911:

> "'I must warn you, Fortune, you are not likely to make many converts in Fanua'.
> 'What, are they cannibals?'
> 'No, no! But they are like children always singing and dancing, and of course immoral. But all the natives are like that. I believe I have told you that the Raratongan language has no words for chastity or for gratitude?'"

With her intuitive perception of the interplay between faith, culture and human relationships, the author brings the central character to a stark realisation. When the Reverend Fortune's one 'convert' attempts suicide because his own personal god has been taken away from him, the missionary soberly reflects:

> "because I loved him so for what he was I could not spend a day without trying to alter him. How dreadful it is that because of our wills we can never love anything without messing it about." (16)

During the nineteenth century when the Christian faith was under attack in Britain from post-Darwinian science and philosophies such as Auguste Comte's Positivism, Methodism was distinctively evangelical in its missionary zeal overseas. Meanwhile the fundraising and administrative tasks at home had increased to support the rapidly expanding work overseas, which by the second half of the nineteenth century embraced considerable educational and medical services. The developments in Methodist mission were paralleled in other denominations: the need for communication and co-operation resulted in the World Missionary Conference of 1910 (Edinburgh) with its slogan "the Evangelisation of the World in this Generation."

We may, then, identify two prominent features of the Methodist overseas mission (in common with many of the other Protestant missions) in the nineteenth and early twentieth centuries: firstly, the imposition of white, British cultural norms, values, organisation and practices along with the 'saving of souls'; and secondly, the negative attitude taken towards the non-Christian religions of the indigenous peoples. Both have contributed to the sustaining of the illusion, held in the west, of the supremacy of white Christianity and the denigration of other cultures, religions and the people who belonged to them.

Of the end of this period Birtwhistle comments:

> "Into this gentle world of steady progress and dedicated service came the war. Printed on paper of steadily deteriorating quality, the Annual Reports of the Society described the effects of the conflagration ..... banks closed, commerce disorganized, missionaries worried about supplies ..... building work had stopped." (17)

The stance appears somewhat parochial in its concern for the minutiae of administration. Birtwhistle's comment that "by far the most important single event in the whole period" was the World Missionary Conference of 1910, confirms the impression of a structure trying doggedly to pursue its aims and operations in a world which was changing around it. The Society Report of 1919 noted: "Nationalism is inclined to range itself against Christianity" - "one of the the most masterly understatements in the whole vast pile of missionary literature" states Birtwhistle.(18) As Geoffrey Moorhouse points out, the missionaries (Catholic and Protestant) had justified their presence in Africa as messengers of gentleness and love; the white men were now seen by Africans to turn against each other.

The loss of white credibility, combined with incipient nationalism and the apparent insensitivity of missionaries returning after the war to black Christian communities which had managed well without white leadership in the interim, were all portents of change.

Moorhouse identifies the main contribution of nineteenth and twentieth century missions to Africa as being agents of the gift of freedom from white supremacy, through the provision of education (many of the black Africans who led their countries to independence after the war were educated in missionary schools) and their pressure on colonial governments to prepare the indigenous people for independence.[19]

In their book The Missionary Myth (1973), Richard and Helen Exley, as agnostics with experience of working in Africa with aid organisations, report their personal discoveries about and responses to the contemporary missionaries in Africa whom they interviewed. They write:

> "The situation in the last twenty years has completely altered and it is perhaps not surprising that the public here has not kept pace with the breadth of this change. Missionaries have been stripped of all power. They have moved from the centre of the stage to the position of servants, and this has ushered in the profoundest psychological changes." (20)

A Methodist missionary agricultural worker in Kenya impressed the Exley's by the way he accepted the authority of an African leader with far less education than himself. He had no doubt about the change in attitude:

> "There have been three eras of missionaries in Kenya. The first were pioneers and dictators, the second paternalists, and the third are here to serve." (21)

Lesslie Newbigin, discussing educational, health and agricultural enterprises, comments that during the period of the dismantling of the colonial empires this part of mission continued in the same pattern despite new labels of "technical assistance" and "development".[22] He notes:

> "One can record a strong movement in the last ten years (1968-1978) away from the idea of service offered by the strong to the weak, towards actions designed to enable the needy and powerless to become aware of their situation, to understand the forces which control and dominate them, and to organize themselves for their own liberation." (23)

Newbigin goes on to discuss the "liberation theology" emerging from Southern and Central America, but for our present purposes it is perhaps more relevant to note the changes taking place in intercultural theology and the new initiatives being taken by those on the receiving end of the nineteenth and twentieth century missions to write <u>their</u> accounts of the history of Christianity. Walter Hollenweger reviews such contributions in a paper in the <u>International Review of Mission</u>, October 1987. The work of two Methodists, Emmanuel Lartey, a Ghanaian, and George Mulrain from Trinidad (both ministers) are of particular interest here. Lartey's study of "Pastoral Counselling in Intercultural Perspective" illustrates in which ways western models of psychology and pastoral care (and of teaching theology) are alien to the African, for whom family and ancestors are more important than emphasis on the individual. In "Theology and Folk Culture", George Mulrain describes "why the theological education which he received in college proved largely irrelevant in the missionary situation in Haiti"; the situation being that the Vaudou folk religion holds elements which are rationally inexplicable but should not be despised.

Both these Methodists are in the special position of being able to "translate" into western academic and theological terms their understanding of that which is of God in the cultures and religious traditions of, what were, receiving countries. They are both to take up theological posts in Birmingham in 1989.

In his contribution to the book Ten Sending Churches (1985), Donald Knighton begins his account of Selly Oak Methodist (Birmingham) by stating that it is a receiving church. A world map kept in the church records regular worshippers from overseas: at the time, he noted, it showed 88 people from 25 different countries.[24] It is important that such invaluable opportunities should be taken by British Christians to listen and learn from people whose experience of the church and Christianity has been gained not only in different cultural settings, but also amongst people of other faiths.

The Overseas Division of the Methodist Church, (MCOD) the Methodist Missionary Society, is entrusted with the initiation and continuance of mission overseas, the continuing relationship of mutual help with the overseas churches in whose life such missionary enterprise has played a part and ecumenical relationships in the field of mission overseas.

> "The Methodist Missionary Society is none other than the Methodist Church itself organised for mission overseas; the members of the Methodist Missionary Society are the members of the Methodist Church and every member of the Methodist Church as such is a member of the Methodist Missionary Society"(25)

It is not possible to be a Methodist and not bear some responsibility for Methodism's relationship with people of other faiths.

A meeting of the Central Committee of the Overseas Division of the Methodist Church in November 1988 reported in the Methodist Recorder(26) provides a useful insight into the current concerns of the Methodist Church in Britain relating to mission. The consideration given to 'Proclamation' is of special interest in that the Reverend Tom Stuckey drew attention to the cultural context of theology and, feeling like "a cannibal about to be eaten by missionaries", he made four affirmations:

> "Our need to come to terms with pluralism (the conversion of all includes our own conversion); commitment to the particularity (a word he chose in preference to uniqueness) of Jesus, and to exploring what the cosmic Christ means in different contexts; the place of the poor and our need to stand where the poor stand in order to hear Jesus clearly; a belief that God is moving before us, that the Gospel is open and inclusive ('unconfined' in the language of Wesley, HP 48) reaching out to all creation."

The issues were recognised to be of fundamental importance to the Committee and "lively contributions" to the debate had to be curtailed for lack of time. The suggestion to set up an inter-divisional consultation on pluralism and the theology of mission was accepted. Later in the proceedings discussion on new initiatives in mission was linked with this proposal. God's power to change could be identified as the keynote of the meeting. The acknowledgement of the implications for all areas of the Church's activities - at home and abroad - may be seen as a positive move towards fresh understanding and interpretation of the theology and praxis of mission by Methodist Christians.

The 'heathen' are no longer at arms length overseas; the observation that there are now more Muslims in Britain than

Methodists[27] highlights the imminent reality of our contemporary religious plurality. The days of dictatorship and paternalism have gone, leaving Christian minorities overseas to deal with the residual resentment, scepticism and dislike which is part of the imperial legacy attached to organized Christianity. The legacy is with us at home in the human form of immigrants and their descendants, whose history and experience have been formed or touched by the British Christian enterprises of the nineteenth and twentieth centuries. The church has not only to confront its own past, but also its present situation in the world in order to discover its contemporary role and the nature of mission.

An honest appraisal of our missionary past is crucial, not only for relations with people of other faiths, but for relations between white, black and brown Christians. As we observed from the church study, issues of colour and culture are interwoven in Methodists' thinking and attitudes to the extent that questions about people of other religions were answered in terms of other colours - Christian and non-Christian, and difference in colour related to divisions of black and white within the church community. Those of us who are white Methodists are only barely beginning to understand how our missionary past has influenced the way we regard people of other colours, faiths and cultures: attitudes of superiority and arrogance, or at best, paternalism, conscious or unconscious, are debilitating, not only for the recipients but also for the purveyors. We have not yet learnt that 'otherness' is not a threat, but a promise, or that diversity is not a weakness, but a strength.

Interfaith dialogue offers a way of learning from the religious experience of others, and also in the process, challenges each of us to examine the very essence of what it means to be a Christian.

2. Ecumenism

Methodism's commitment to the ecumenical movement has been significant, both nationally and internationally. It is peculiarly suited to this task through its own experience of piecemeal amalgamation and the eventual union of a variety of Methodist churches; The Methodist Church was formed by the Methodist Church Union Act 1929 and the Deed of Union of 1932 defined the constitution and doctrinal standards of the united church.[28]

The achievement of this unity carries the long and tortuous history of a problem left unresolved by the founder of the movement. John Wesley lived and died an Anglican, having established a large network of Methodist societies throughout Britain and Ireland. Less than two years before his death, when visiting the society in Dublin he recorded in his Journal:

> "I met the society and explained to them at large the original design of the Methodists, viz., not to be a distinct party, but to stir up all parties, Christians or Heathens, to worship God in Spirit and in truth; but the Church of England in particular; to which they belonged from the beginning." (29)

It seems that whilst never abandoning this principle, his tireless efforts to establish, nurture and direct local societies to function as distinctive groups of Christians, worked in practice to the opposite effect. The class meeting, the appointment of lay leaders and preachers, an itinerant ministry, and later the ordination of Methodists by Wesley (who was not a Bishop) to minister in America, were important organisational features of Methodism during Wesley's lifetime which marked it off from the Church of England. Nevertheless, doctrinally and sacramentally Wesley was Anglican in his views.(30) As Henry D. Rack explains in his account of Wesleyan Methodism 1849-1902:

> "Refusing to regard Methodism as a 'church', Wesley did not feel called upon to develop the new theory of the church which his practice might otherwise have required. Later Methodism clearly was a church, or rather a group of churches ..... a self sufficient religious body, and not a dependent society." (31)

During the nineteenth century two main groupings emerged. Robert Currie in Methodism Divided: A Study of the Sociology of Ecumenism clarifies the distinctions:

> "Wesleyan catholicity - its doctrines of ministry and sacrament, its stress on order, its hierarchical rule - suggest many Roman analogies; reformed Methodism's doctrine of spiritual equality, its stress on evangelism, its system of representative government, have obvious parallels in Protestantism as a whole." (32)

The opening doctrinal statement of the Deed of Union indicates the compromise reached: (the whole statement is presented in Appendix B)

> "The Methodist Church claims and cherishes its place in the Holy Catholic Church which is the Body of Christ. It rejoices in the inheritance of the Apostolic Faith and loyally accepts the fundamental principles of the historic creeds and of the Protestant Reformation. It ever remembers that in the Providence of God Methodism was raised up to spread Scriptural Holiness through the land by the proclamation of the Evangelical Faith and declares its unfaltering resolve to be true to its Divinely appointed mission." (33)

Robert Currie's thesis is that ecumenism is always in part a response to adversity, and more specifically to numerical decline.[34] He supports this with a detailed study of the development of the Methodist Church.

> "When frontal growth, i.e. the acquisition of new members by the normal processes of recruitment and enrolment fails, the organization seeks to achieve its goal by lateral growth, i.e. amalgamation with other organisations in possession of membership and resources of their own." (35)

Methodist writers such as J. M. Turner do not happily accept this. He comments:

> "The theory may be vulnerable, while much of the hard evidence lying underneath it is much more intractable." (36)

Currie goes on to assert that the efforts towards Methodist/ Anglican union in particular, and among Christian Churches in general, are due to the same stimulus - adverse conditions. Ecumenism, he says:

> "arises out of decline and secularization, but fails to deal with either. ..... A more critical appraisal is overdue, for the hope that ecumenicalism will be the salvation of Christianity seems illusory." (37)

Again, this is disputed by Methodist writers. Strawson says:

> "the movement towards unity among the Churches has been strongly supported in Methodism, not chiefly because the future of separate denominations seems so insecure, but because it can claim strong biblical support and because it seems to be a necessary prerequisite for the effective proclamation of Christ in the twentieth century." (38)

This view is echoed by Rupert Davies:

> "It is true that, since the Churches have seen the decline in their size and influence, many Christians have urged the need for ecumenism for the sake of strength, but the original and continuing rationale of ecumenism is biblical, theological and evangelistic." (39)

Methodism has always carried within its community those who place the highest value on the tradition of the church (e.g. the Wesleyans), those who valued Scripture as the highest authority (e.g. the Bible Christians), and those for whom present Spirit overruled either (e.g. the Holiness Movement); it thus recognises that the valuing of one does not preclude a place for the others and is in this reminiscent of the unity and diversity of the early Christian community.(40) In holding on to firstly, the belief in one catholic church, secondly the primacy of Scripture, and thirdly the priesthood of all believers (on whom are bestowed the gifts of the Spirit evidenced by the 'fruit'),(41) in such a way as to make developments in all directions possible, Methodism has safeguarded Wesley's intention that the Methodists should be 'the friends of all and the enemies of none'.

In practical terms the ecumenical tradition has led to a large number of co-operative ventures between the Protestant churches through Areas of Ecumenical Experiment, with shared use of premises, Anglican/Methodist schools, shared chaplaincies, joint appointments and church centres. With the Roman Catholic Church, joint services, exchanges of pulpit and Lent Groups are now established practices in many areas. The future of co-operative ventures will not be affected by the failure of the Anglican/Methodist Unity Proposals in 1983, largely attributable to the unresolved issue of ordination.(42)

In fact, the new "Inter Church Process" initiative appears to have developed to fill the vacuum on a much broader basis. "Not Strangers but Pilgrims" involves twenty-eight Churches in England, Scotland and Wales, including the Roman Catholic Church in England and Wales and in Scotland, the mainline Protestant churches, the Religious Society of Friends and the

New Testament Assembly. A meeting at Swanwick in 1987 produced a report and a declaration:

> "Our churches must now move from co-operation to clear commitment to each other, in search of the unity for which Christ prayed, and in common evangelism and service of the world." (43)

"Ecumenical Instruments" have been developed for implementing the sharing of resources for common witness and ministry at local church level.

> "All this depends upon a new vision of life together: not one monolithic church but rather a family gathering together the gifts and diversities developed while churches worked apart."

The closing comment of this section of the four-page advertising feature on "Not Strangers but Pilgrims" in the Methodist Recorder 2 February 1989 says:

> "Once there was rivalry. Now, convinced of the insufficiency of all our insights to exhaust the mystery of God, we must look to one another to fill up what we lack on our own. We must take one another seriously, be patient with disagreements and hold on to a commitment to persevere as God's gift of unity is more fully received."

Read from an inter-faith as well as an intra-faith perspective, the statement is also viable and offers immense possibilities. Can even all the Christians "exhaust the mystery of God"? The four principles of dialogue adopted for the 'wider ecumenism' appear to be central also to Christian ecumenism.

It is suggested that the significance of the ecumenical movement for inter-faith dialogue lies in two areas. Firstly, dialogue between the churches has formed a natural precursor to dialogue between Christians and non-Christians. The process of discovering what is held in common, identifying areas of difference and being open to what they have to offer, holding the tension and moving forward with resolve, have been learnt through experience at local church level, in the British Council of Churches and the World Council of Churches. Methodist initiatives in interfaith dialogue have, as we saw in the last chapter, been largely channelled through ecumenical agencies - the BCC and WCC. Secondly, the ecumenical movement has involved Christians all over the world, and the world has become the proper focus of attention: a global vision has complemented parochial concerns.

Hans Küng's statement puts the position clearly:

> "There will be no peace among the people of this world without peace among the world religions.
> "There will be no peace among the world religions without peace among the Christian Churches." (44)

'Peace' does not necessarily imply unity, and unity, as Methodists well know, does not imply uniformity; it means accepting and living with diversity.

If Currie's warnings are heeded - that ecumenism does not halt declining memberships and provide a stronger base for evangelism and the spread of Christianity - then "a more critical appraisal" is indeed overdue. In our contemporary situation that appraisal must take serious account of the presence and nature of the other world religions as well as of Christian theology. Some Methodists have been amongst those keen to acknowledge this by their participation at local, national and international level in ecumenical ventures: local Interfaith Councils, the Committee on Relations with People of Other Faiths (BCC, set up in 1978) and the Sub Unit of the WCC on Dialogue with People of Living Faiths and Ideologies (established in 1970). The Methodist Church established its own Committee on Relations with People of Other Faiths in 1983 and in 1988 appointed its first full time minister to work nationally among those of other faiths, establishing lines of communication between the Christian Church and other world religions.[(45)] In Birmingham, the location of the church study, there is an ecumenical appointment, to which Methodists are party, of an Indian-born Christian with a brief for pastoral work amongst newly arrived Hindus, Muslims and Sikhs; he is responsible to a committee chaired by Lesslie Newbigin. The Chairman of the Birmingham District of the Methodist Church is encouraging the ministers and others in the district to identify the practical, pastoral and theological concerns of working in religiously plural areas with a view to sharing experience and ideas on multi-faith matters. Many of these Methodists are accustomed to working with other Christians in their localities: ecumenical considerations necessarily feature in local institutional initiatives where Protestant and Catholic denominations have established working relationships on issues that are recognised as having implications beyond individual congregations.

In view of the interweaving of intra-faith and inter-faith dialogue and encounter at world, national and local level, it is not surprising that the participants of the church survey were drawn to thinking about ecumenical involvement when asked about relations with other religions. That matters appear to be moving along the lines of practical commitment first and attention to theological and doctrinal matters subsequently, may also offer a pattern for relationships between different faith communities based on the four principles.

However, a strong stimulus to Methodist involvement in unity among the churches in Britain has been to create an effective basis for evangelism, and this has been as much a reason for concern in overseas mission this century, as in home mission. Here, in ecumenism, as in the area of overseas mission, we are brought back to the central question of Methodist relations with people of other faiths. Is a united base for evangelism to be used for proselytising, to add numbers to the Church or will it produce a new model of dialogical mission deriving from Christians' own intra-faith experience of the dialogical process?

We now turn to our third formative characteristic of Methodism: the particular contribution of Methodism defined by John Wesley - the doctrine of Christian Perfection (Scriptural Holiness).

3. Christian Perfection

Wesley said of Christian Perfection, or Scriptural Holiness, that it was:

> "the grand deposition which God has lodged with the people called Methodists; and for the sake of propagating this chiefly He appeared to have raised us up." (46)

In a life spanning most of the eighteenth century (1703-1791), John Wesley wrote hundreds of sermons, treatises, pamphlets, letters, hymns and a Journal. There is, therefore, ample material from which to draw information - and a variety of conclusions.

> "I want to know one thing - the way to heaven; how to land safe on that happy shore God Himself has condescended to teach the way; for this very end he came from heaven. He hath written it down in a book. O give me that book! At any price, give me the book of God! I have it: here is knowledge enough for me. Let me be homo unius libri."(47)

Rupert Davies, in the opening pages of "The People called Methodists: 'Our Doctrine'" draws attention to this statement and finds it, as a clear affirmation of Wesley's biblical theological method, substantiated throughout the Sermons and Treatises. Davies uses this as evidence to prove that Wesley's theology was biblical theology, not the theology of experience.(48) Yet Wesley closes the Preface to the Forty-four Sermons, just quoted, by saying:

> "For, how far is love, even with many wrong opinions, to be preferred before truth itself without love! ... May He prepare us for the knowledge of all truth, by filling our hearts with all His love, and with all joy and peace in believing!" (49)

In between he reveals his purposes for writing the Sermons: to guard those who are "just setting their faces toward heaven" from "formality, from mere outside religion"; and to warn those who know "the religion of the heart", in case they "make void the law". To Wesley, religion is both "scriptural" and "experimental"; holiness is outward and inward; Christian perfection is perfect love.

It is necessary to attempt a simplified broad outline of Wesley's "way to heaven" to place Scriptural Holiness, or Christian Perfection, in the scheme. We follow Rupert Davies' exposition in "Our Doctrines".(50) Man is born in a state of Original Sin, due to the Fall of Adam, since which time "all the blessings which God hath bestowed upon man are of His mere grace, bounty or favour" (prevenient grace; Sermon "On Faith").

"Grace is the source, faith the condition of salvation."("On Faith") Repentance (i.e. acknowledgement of sinful, hopeless state) usually comes before faith, but is not a condition of salvation in the way that faith is. Repentance shows itself in the performance of good and righteous deeds - which do not give salvation, either. The faith which brings salvation has two stages: firstly, "it is a faith in Christ: Christ, and God through Christ, are the proper objects of it"; the second stage is reached when a man is able to testify to this conviction that "the life I now live, I live by faith in the Son of God, who loved me and gave himself for me." ("On Faith"). A man can know he is saved (assurance) and communicate to others that he is saved (witness). Faith brings justification, (being pardoned for sin) and the New Birth. Sanctification begins from the moment of justification - or as Davies puts it, "the helpless sinner is on the way to becoming a saint".(51)

Now we can return to Scriptural Holiness. In one of his last Sermons ("On the Wedding Garment", 1790) Wesley wrote, "By faith we are saved from sin and made holy". Holiness he defines as keeping the commandments, particularly the Great Commandments to love God with all your heart and your neighbour as yourself; this is the same as having "the mind that was in Christ" and "walking as Christ walked" and is perfect love, Christian perfection. There is no contradiction, says Wesley, in his two statements "By grace ye are saved through faith" and "without holiness no man shall see the Lord."(52)

Wesley's doctrine of Christian Perfection was far from

popular.[53] As he himself wrote:

> "There is scarce any expression in holy writ, which has given more offence than this ..... whosoever preaches perfection (as the phrase is), that is asserts that it is attainable in this life, runs great hazard of being accounted by them worse than a heathen man or a publican."

The most strident objections were made to that part of the doctrine which claimed that once a man is justified, he does not sin.

> "Christians are saved in this world from all sin, from all unrighteousness; that they are now in such a sense perfect, as not to commit sin, and to be freed from evil thoughts and evil tempers." (54)

Wesley was unable to prove it experimentally, but held the view was Scriptural and refused to retract it. Davies gives up grappling with the idea and concludes Wesley "must have been mistaken". Jean Orcibal, contributing to the same volume of A History of the Methodist Church in Great Britain, gives an interesting and different appraisal:

> "It was surely in 1740 a really revolutionary achievement to complete the doctrine of justification by faith by means of the teaching of the synoptic gospels on sanctification, and even more to preach to Protestants the ideal of perfection ..... What could be bolder in the Age of Enlightenment than to rehabilitate that mysticism which was the consequence of perfection ..... Through it Wesley has perhaps contributed more than anyone to the survival [in American and Continental Protestantism] of the appeal of the inner life and of the belief in the possibility of holiness or 'pure love of God'". (55)

Wesley derived much insight from Roman Catholic authors such as Thomas à Kempis. Works by Brother Lawrence, Fénelon, Mme Guyon and Antoinette Bourignon, for example, were published by Wesley as part of his Christian Library for the benefit of the lay preachers in particular and the Methodist people in general.[56] Gordon Rupp comments that while the Christian Library "never really caught on", the influence on Wesley himself of this literature was important:

> "his doctrine of perfect love owed much to this spiritual theology and was, as a result, richer, more complex, more intricate than the subsequent literature of 'holiness' in nineteenth century evangelism." (57)

John M. Turner, drawing on Albert Outler's appraisal of Wesley's view of perfection, also points out the influence of the Eastern Fathers. Wesley included the Homilies of Macarius the Egyptian in the Christian Library and the concept here of perfection as a process, rather than a state, contributed to the development of Wesley's doctrine.

> "Thus the ancient and Eastern tradition of holiness as disciplined love became fused in Wesley's mind with his own Anglican position of holiness as aspiring love producing what he felt was a distinctive contribution to Christian thinking." (58)

William Strawson identifies two strands of theological tradition arising from the doctrine of Christian Perfection:[59] one is reflected in the work of men like F.W. Platt and R. Newton Flew, and endeavoured to interpret the doctrine in the light of contemporary ideas of human nature and responsibilities. The other, represented by men such as Thomas Champness and Samuel Chadwick, strengthened the basis of Methodist 'enthusiasm' and the longing for the 'second blessing'; it found expression in the Holiness Conventions and Cliff College. This tradition emphasized that a high standard of conduct cannot be obtained without the aid of the Holy Spirit and maintained an emphasis on evangelism and personal witness. The record of the Convention for the Promotion of Scriptural Holiness at Brighton in 1875 provides a useful picture of the movement. The 'Call' issued by the committee under the chairmanship of R. Pearsall Smith, points out that in many continental countries and America such meetings had been held:

> "for the sole purpose of gaining, under the guidance of the Holy Spirit, a truly Scriptural experience of sanctification, and power in service ..... Beyond their largest expectations or even hopes, the Lord has manifested Himself to His waiting people." (60)

The Review of the proceedings, quoting from Friends Quarterly Examiner, says:

> "It is in making experimental that which we have held doctrinally, that the whole vigour of our spiritual life consists: and this is the key to the rapid spread of this movement for the promotion of Scriptural holiness". (61)

Samuel Chadwick criticised the church for its intellectualism, 'modern' views of the Bible and failure to seek 'the second blessing'.[(62)] Cliff College, with which he was associated, continues its work of training evangelists for "A lifetime of service in the Kingdom of God".

Strawson hails Hugh Price Hughes as the person who fused the holiness tradition and social concern. In his earlier ministry he was actively associated with the Holiness Conventions led by Pearsall Smith,[(63)] later saw a need for political involvement and became one of the leaders of the Forward Movement. John M. Turner describes this as "the last great attempt to reach those alienated from all the churches" in its efforts to provide centres of evangelism and social amelioration - "the sacrament and the soup-ladle hand in hand".[(64)]

But let us return to trace Strawson's first strand of holiness in Methodism. In what he describes as "the most scholarly and competent study of this doctrine" in The Idea of Perfection in Christian Theology (1934), Flew "places the Methodist doctrine in the context of Catholic tradition" and identifies Perfection with Spirituality.[65] Flew, along with Russell Maltby, J. Alexander Findlay, T. S. Gregory (who became a Roman Catholic) and the young Leslie Weatherhead, was part of a movement in the 1920s called the "Fellowship of the Kingdom". Turner says of them:

> "they were able to contain a rich catholic spirituality with an intense concern to follow 'the historical Jesus' as he had been revealed to them by the Protestant biblical scholarship which they had studied." (66)

Strawson says of Maltby and Weatherhead that they had "an extraordinary grasp of the reality of Jesus".[67] Their emphasis is on personal experience and is open to charges of 'blatant individualism' and 'anti-intellectualism' - that is, to those who feel individualism is 'wrong' and intellectualism is 'right' in matters of religion. Leslie Weatherhead (1893-1976) makes a convincing case against these criticisms in his book The Transforming Friendship:

> "He loved me, and gave Himself up for me ..... This is not a narrow creed. If it is egotism, it is a higher egotism, for it is an egotism which is the only basis of altruism. And the quality of the one will determine the strength of the other."
>
> "Jesus did not demand intellectual assent to a creed. He did not question Peter as to whether he was sound on the inspiration of the Old Testament. He said 'Follow me'. Peter accepted the gift of a transforming friendship with Jesus. Then he made his own theology afterwards out of his own experience." (68)

Having the clarity and simplicity of one of the greatest Methodist preachers of this century, Weatherhead goes on to explain:

"The only way I know of practising the presence of God is by practising the presence of Jesus, who makes God credible and real." (69)

Of the presence of God he had no doubt:

"There is a sense in which every man is an incarnation of God. Divinity is not in a different category of thought from humanity." (70)

Leslie Weatherhead was not only a preacher and pastor, but also a channel of spiritual healing. The intuitive imagination which he drew on to realise the presence of God extended also to his relationships with other people. Recognising that:

"There is with all real friends, the kind of communion of spirit which can be expressed only in long silences, when soul to some extent does seem to penetrate soul,"

he knew that Jesus "comes to us below the levels plumbed by our most intimate friends."(71)

In Key Next Door, a collection of sermons published in 1959, he writes:

"I am quite sure that our minds go to incalculable depths and join up with other minds, and ultimately with the universal mind, and the truth that is not science so much as wisdom, and is not so much outwardly conveyed as inwardly revealed, is of far greater importance." (72)

Considerable attention has been given to Leslie Weatherhead, though not enough to explore all the implications of his teaching, or to express the quality of love for Jesus and people which permeate his work. While he is firmly in Wesley's 'biblical' and 'experimental' tradition, what he had to say also has connecting-points with Carl Gustav Jung and Teilhard de Chardin referred to in Chapter I, and it might also be suggested, with some aspects of the New Age teaching. He was a pioneer in relating psychology and psychoanalysis to

Christianity through his writings and practical involvement in healing and counselling.[73] He was in favour of "serious psychic research",[74] and published a work on Reincarnation, finding it compatible with Christian Teaching.[75] He was not always in tune with the establishment! Weatherhead also forms a link between Wesley's Scriptural Holiness and contemporary movements in Methodism. The current President of Conference, Rev. Dr. Richard G. Jones, is quoted in the Methodist Recorder of 5 January 1989 as discovering in his tours around the country:

> "a much greater sense of the spiritual dimension to life, which was most noticeable in both the ministry and in the churches yearning for a deeper spirituality, for retreats, for the healing ministry and renewed sacramental life."

It is possible that in the vast, largely uncharted area of personal spiritual experience, (beyond the great mystical writers like Julian of Norwich, St. John of the Cross, Meister Eckhart, Thomas Merton etc.), boundaries between the world religions may be crossed. "Dialogue must be based on personal religious experience and firm truth claims" says Paul Knitter.[76] Hans Küng in Christianity and the World Religions poses the questions:

> "Isn't religion, above all - before it is doctrine and morality, rites and institutions - religious experience?"
>
> "Is spiritual experience everywhere the same?" (77)

We shall not know unless we are willing to find out.

Paul Tillich also argues for inter-religious discussion on the basis of a particular religious commitment to the universal question of the meaning of life:

> "The way is to penetrate into the depth of one's own religion, in devotion, thought and action. In the depth

> of every living religion there is a point at which the religion itself loses its importance, and that to which it points breaks through its particularity, elevating it to spiritual freedom and with it to a vision of the spiritual presence in other expressions of the ultimate meaning of man's existence. This is what Christianity must see in the present encounter of the world religions." (78)

So it may be that our 'grand deposition' of the doctrine of Scriptural Holiness seen as a source to be reinterpreted and applied in the current "spiritual renewal" in Methodism, may also be the most truly Methodist contribution to interfaith dialogue. It comes as no surprise to discover that Leslie Weatherhead, the man who talks of Jesus as his personal Friend, answers the question of his Sermon "Is Christianity the Only Way to God?" by a firm 'No'. On the basis of his own religious experience, and of working for some years in Madras, his thoughts on the subject are: God can be found in other religions; God's love and care is all-embracing; our own interpretation of Christ may be enriched by the teaching in other faiths, for other faiths contain truth. Yet, for him, "no other path up the mountain of truth leads towards the summit so directly, or comes so nearly to its goal as Christianity" and Jesus was "filled with the spirit of God more than any man".(79)

> "We shall never really know the fullness of Christ, or what Christ is really like, until all the nations have brought the treasures of their thought and insight to the final and complete revelation. Christ has revealed God, but who shall reveal Christ?" (80)

Christian Perfection pertains to individuals, not the corporate body of the Church; it is essentially the path of experience - directed by Scripture and nurtured through the fellowship and "means of grace" of the worshipping community - yet from beginning to end a personal spiritual journey of realising the presence of God and living according to the insight gained from that experience. Wesley realised that for eighteenth century Christians, just as for first century Christians, personal religious experience is central. We have seen the holiness thread re-emerging this century in the life and teaching of Leslie Weatherhead - who was no less criticised for some of his insights than Wesley was for his doctrine of Perfection. On the basis of his awareness of living in the Presence, through the friendship of Jesus, Weatherhead was able to recognise the Presence in people of other faiths. Scriptural holiness is perfect love; it is living the Great commandments, in which loving your neighbour and loving yourself follow loving God. It is a gift, the acceptance of which is the basis for dialogue with people of other faiths.

Of one stage in his spiritual journey of "passing over" and "coming back", John S. Dunne writes:

> "I decided I would pass over to other religions to see how God comes among us and how we walk with God. There is an experience that is common to the great religions, I came to believe, an experience of human wholeness, as in the formula 'with all your heart, and with all your soul, and with all your might', but there is a difference of insight into the experience".(81)

Coming back to Christianity he continued his "spiritual adventure" finding it more and more a journey with God into solitude and back into the human circle.

> "Each step of the journey begins as a kindling of the heart and ends as illumining the mind." (82)

As Wesley put it in the quotation above (page 96)

> "May He prepare us for the knowledge of all truth, by filling our hearts with all His love."

4. Summary

The Methodist overseas missionary movement of the nineteenth and much of the twentieth century, involved as it was with colonialism and white domination, not only spread Christianity throughout many parts of Africa, Asia and China, but also left a legacy at home of attitudes of superiority towards and disdain for non-Christian peoples. Despite the high hopes of the missionary drive around the turn of the nineteenth century, the world was not evangelised in that generation; religiously plural societies are a fact of life and will, in all probability remain so. In the meeting of different faiths and cultures, the distinction between home and overseas mission becomes blurred and Methodism, we noted in the previous chapter, is beginning to recognise that the theology of mission needs reappraisal. There is a need to listen to the new generations of overseas Christians in order to understand the relationship between faith and cultural norms and practices and subsequently to reflect on the realities of Christian practice in Britain.

Methodist commitment to its own internal, British and World ecumenism has provided useful experience in dialogue and living with diversity at all levels of church activity. Many people have had their knowledge and vision broadened by sharing others' traditions and joint ventures in service to the community have been productive. It may also be, however, that the obsession with ecclesiology which has dominated Methodist history has distracted attention from missiology and therefore also in more recent years from developing a theology of interfaith dialogue. The experience of the intra-faith dialogical process could now be positively applied to relations with other religions - given the will to do so.

Our first selected element of Methodism concerned the world, the second Christian churches in Britain and the third brought our attention to the individual and the heart of the original Methodist revival: Christian Perfection. John Wesley, like Jesus, was not concerned with dismantling the religious structure he was born into, or with establishing a new religion: he was committed to "stirring up" individual men and women to be holy, to receive, reflect on and live the perfect love of God. Methodism emphasises that religion is centrally about experiencing the presence of God: this was observed in the Holiness Movement of the nineteenth century and in the twentieth century through the identification of Scriptural Holiness with Sprituality. Leslie Weatherhead forms a bridge into present Methodist interfaith relations: by living in awareness of the Presence, we are able to recognise the Presence in people of other religions. We may also be able to share insights into life.

-oOo-

References

(1) N. Allen Birtwhistle, "Methodist Missions", in A History of the Methodist Church in Great Britain, Vol. 3, p.1.

(2) Ibid, p.2.

(3) Ibid, p.1.

(4) Ibid, p.36.

(5) Ibid, p.106.

(6) Jeffrey Harris and Peter Jarvis, Counting to Some Purpose, p.5.

(7) Birtwhistle, op. cit., p.9.

(8) Ibid, p.10.

(9) The slave trade was abolished by Act of Parliament in England in 1807 (Stephen Neill, A History of Christian Missions, p.260); the full emancipation of the slaves in British West Indian territories occurred in 1838 (Birtwhistle, op. cit., p.51).

(10) Kenneth Cracknell, Towards a New Relationship, p.23.

(11) Ibid, p.19.

(12) Birtwhistle, op. cit., p.71.

(13) Cracknell, op. cit., p.20.

(14) Stephen Neill, A History of Christian Missions, pp. 251-255.

(15) Ibid, p.254, quoting from Professor Latourette's A History of the Expansion of Christianity, Vol. V, p.223.

(16) Sylvia Townsend Warner, Mr. Fortune's Maggot, pp. 3, 194.

(17) Birtwhistle, op. cit., pp.114-115.

(18) Ibid, p.115.

(19) Geoffrey Moorhouse, The Missionaries: Chapter 17 "Paradise Lost" on the changes following World War II; his conclusions on the missionary contribution pp.334-335.

(20) Richard and Helen Exley, The Missionary Myth, p.5.

(21) Ibid, p.123.

(22) Lesslie Newbigin, The Open Secret, p.104.

(23) Ibid, p.105.

(24) Donald Knighton, "Selly Oak Methodist Church, Birmingham", in Michael Griffiths, Editor, Ten Sending Churches, p.92.

(25) The Constitutional Practice and Discipline of The Methodist Church, Vol. 2, pp. 679-680.

(26) Jan Pickard, "Words and Actions" in The Methodist Recorder 10th November 1988.

(27) British Council of Churches, Relations with Peoples of Other Faiths: Guidelines for Dialogue (revised edition 1983), p.2.

(28) The Constitutional Practice and Discipline of the Methodist Church, Vol. 2, pp.204-5.

(29) The Journal of John Wesley: A Selection, ed. Elisabeth Jay, p.247.

(30) When asked in what points Methodists differed from the Church of England, Wesley answered: "To the best of my knowledge, in none. The doctrines we preach are the doctrines of the Church of England; indeed the fundamental doctrines of the Church, clearly laid down, both in her Prayers, Articles and Homilies." Ibid, p.45.

(31) Henry D. Rack, "Wesleyan Methodism 1849-1902" in A History of the Methodist Church in Britain, Vol. 3, p. 157.

(32) Robert Currie, Methodism Divided: A Study in the Sociology of Ecumenism, p.5.

(33) The Constitutional Practice and Discipline of the Methodist Church, Vol. 2, pp.225-226.

(34) Currie, op. cit., p.14.

(35) Ibid, p.86.

(36) John M. Turner, "Methodism in England 1900-1932", in A History of the Methodist Church in Great Britain, Vol. 3, p.321.

(37) Currie, op. cit., p.361.

(38) William Strawson, "Methodist Theology 1850-1950", in A History of the Methodist Church in Great Britain, Vol. 3, p.223.

(39) Rupert Davies, "Since 1932", in A History of the Methodist Church in Great Britain, Vol. 3, p.372.

(40) James Dunn, Unity and Diversity in the New Testament: the whole of the book is concerned with demonstrating the relatively small core of unity in the beliefs, preaching and practices of the earliest Christians amid the wide diversity; Dunn examines the way in which the common core effected limits on the diversity and the way in which Christianity developed in response to the situations in which it found itself.

(41) The doctrinal standards of The Methodist Church are contained in the Deed of Union and presented in The Constitutional Practice and Discipline of the Methodist Church, Vol. 2, pp.225-226. See Appendix B.

(42) The Ministry of the Whole People of God: a report presented to the 1986 Methodist Conference by the Faith and Order Committee, par. 006.

(43) Methodist Recorder, 2 February 1989.

(44) Hans Küng, Christianity and the World Religions, p.443.

(45) The Methodist Recorder, 29 September 1988. See also pp.65-66 above.

(46) The Letters of John Wesley, Vol. VIII, p.238.

(47) John Wesley, Preface to The Forty-Four Sermons, p.vi.

(48) Rupert Davies, "The People Called Methodists: 'Our Doctrine'" in A History of the Methodist Church in Great Britain, Volume 1, p.149.

(49) John Wesley, Preface to The Forty-Four Sermons, p.vii.

(50) Rupert Davies, op. cit., pp.145-180.

(51) Ibid, p.164.

(52) Wesley's Sermons Vol. 3, CXX "On the Wedding Garment", pp.302-303.

(53) Ibid, pp.168-191; John Walsh, "Methodism at the End of the Eighteenth Century" in A History of the Methodist Church in Great Britain, Volume 1, pp. 290-291.

(54) John Wesley's Forty-Four Sermons, XXXV "Christian Perfection", pp.457, 476.

(55) Jean Orcibal, "The Theological Originality of John Wesley and Continental Spirituality" in A History of the Methodist Church in Great Britain, Volume 1, pp.110-111.

(56) Ibid, p.93.

(57) Gordon Rupp, Introduction to A History of the Methodist Church in Great Britain, Volume 1, p.xxxi.

(58) John M. Turner, Conflict and Reconciliation, p.50, referring to Albert Outler John Wesley, Oxford University Press, 1964.

A useful summary of the main themes of Macarius deriving from Gregory of Nyssa is to be found in A History of Christian Spirituality Vol.I, Editor Louis Bouyer, pp.373-380. A sympathetic account of John Wesley's contribution to this history is given in Vol.III, pp.184-193. Bouyer concludes the section with the comment: "no-one did so much to rebuild the bridges on the spiritual plane between Catholicism (old and new) and a renewed Protestantism".

(59) William Strawson, "Methodist Theology 1850-1950" in A History of the Methodist Church in Great Britain, Volume 3, p.225.

(60) The Convention for the Promotion of Scriptural Holiness, 1875, p.5.

(61) Ibid, p.416.

(62) Strawson, op. cit., pp.228-229.

(63) Ibid, pp. 229-231.

(64) John M. Turner, "Methodism in England 1900-1932", in A History of the Methodist Church in Great Britain, Volume 3, pp.311-312. Turner identifies this as the basis of the central missions and notes that in the early years of the twentieth century, the Leeds mission organised classes in Theology, New Testament Greek, domestic economy and cricket!

(65) Strawson, op. cit., pp.226-227.

(66) Turner, "Methodism in England 1900-1932", p.319.

(67) Strawson, op. cit., p.217.

(68) Leslie Weatherhead, The Transforming Friendship, pp.112-113; p.31.

(69) Ibid., p.46.

(70) Ibid., p.125.

(71) Ibid., pp.64-66.

(72) Leslie Weatherhead, Key Next Door, p.148.

(73) His published works included such titles as Psychology and Life, Psychology in Service of the Soul and Psychology, Religion and Healing.

(74) Leslie Weatherhead, Key Next Door, p.243.

(75) Leslie Weatherhead, The Case for Reincarnation; M. C. Peto, Surrey, 7th Impression 1979; a lecture given to the City Temple Literary Society in 1957.

(76) Paul Knitter, No Other Name?, p.207.

(77) Hans Küng, Christianity and the World Religions, p.168.

(78) Paul Tillich, Christianity and the Encounter of the World Religions, p.97.

(79) Leslie Weatherhead, Key Next Door, p.154.

(80) Ibid, pp.156-157.

(81) John S. Dunne, Reasons of the Heart, pp.149-150.

(82) Ibid, p.152.

CHAPTER IV

METHODIST THEOLOGY AND INTERFAITH DIALOGUE

Throughout this work we have been engaged in dialogue. In the first chapter this was a dialogue with the contemporary realities of our world and with the Bible. The second chapter examined the Methodist Church's dialogue with people of other faiths in Britain. The uncertain and confused picture which emerged led us to probe some characteristic features of Methodism, past and present, in an effort to understand the situation and identify areas where change is indicated. Dialogue with other religions thus also involves us in an encounter with our history in the light of our current awareness and responsibilities to the future. In flowing beyond the boundaries of our own Christian understanding of the God/man/world relationship, we are returned by the tide to the freshly washed substance of our own beach and view it from a different perspective. Such a movement has been made and discussed by two Methodist ministers, Kenneth Cracknell and Wesley Ariarajah.

1. The Contribution of Kenneth Cracknell

Kenneth Cracknell for ten years, from 1978-88, served as Secretary to the BCC Committee for Relations with People of Other Faiths and Associate Secretary of the Conference for World Mission of the BCC. He is now tutor at Wesley House, Cambridge and currently edits Discernment, a Christian Journal of Inter-Religious Encounter, published quarterly by the Committee for Relations with People of Other Faiths since 1986. He is a major British Methodist exponent of interfaith dialogue and encounter and, as a pioneer in the field, has been largely responsible for introducing to a wider audience the issues raised by the institutional churches at world and national level through his own commitment to the value and necessity of developing new Christian relations with people of other faiths. Whilst Secretary of the BCC Committee for Relations with People of Other Faiths Cracknell wrote Why Dialogue?, (published 1980), described as a first British Comment on Guidelines on Dialogue, the document produced by the WCC Sub-Unit on Dialogue with People of Living Faiths and Ideologies (DFI). Why Dialogue? introduces the work of the DFI in the context of changes in the world: pluralist societies, renewed missionary impetus in other religions such as Islam, the effects of secularization, and contemporary political and ideological struggles.

The WCC document is welcomed, firstly, for its commitment to "an integrity of response to the call of the risen Christ to be witnesses to him in all the world" in its exploration of the relationships between 'mission', 'evangelism' and 'dialogue'.(1) Choosing to focus attention on the Bible criteria for interfaith encounter and dialogue, as being "the question most near the lives of our ordinary congregations" in Britain,(2) Cracknell explores the scriptural evidence. He finds in Paul a paradigm for dialogue, spending as he did "two years and three months in the activity described as 'reasoning and persuading'" in Ephesus, both in the synagogue and the Hall of Tyrannus, finding ways of expressing the faith in other cultural settings.(3) Cracknell concludes:

> "Dialogue with people of other faiths and ideologies is misunderstood if it is presented as the only way of mission or if it is represented as being complacent and tolerant in the face of evil nonsense. But, with the example of Paul before us we may equally conclude, in the strongest possible way, that evangelism is distorted if it is presented as happening only by monologue, by one-way proclamation." (4)

Cracknell takes Acts 14:16-17 ("In past generations he allowed all the nations to walk in their own ways; yet he did not leave himself without witness.") as proof that:

> "as far as the Acts of the Apostles are concerned all is not total darkness in the heathen world." (5)

He also draws on Peter's encounter with Cornelius (Acts 10 and 11; see pp.23-24) to emphasise the fundamental guidance for Christians in their attitude to people of other faiths in that "God shows no partiality".(6)

Turning to the Old Testament, Cracknell raises the problems surrounding the concept of 'election', which has been distorted, he says, to support the dictum "outside the church, no salvation". Attention is drawn to "the cosmic covenant".(7)

> "It is perhaps our characteristic preoccupation with redemption, with 'saving acts' and 'salvation-history' that makes us miss so often the biblical feeling for God as universal creator and sustainer." (8)

Addressing the question of whether God has actually revealed himself to anyone outside the covenant people, Cracknell refers to eight passages(9) which support the "staightforward interpretation of Malachi 1:11 (that it refers to Gentiles, not diaspora Jews):

> "For from the rising of the sun to its setting my name is great among the nations, and in every place incense is offered to my name, and a pure offering; for my name is great among the nations, says the Lord of hosts."

Why Dialogue? has been summarised in some detail because the biblical groundwork shows clearly the 'back to base' response of the Protestant Churches and also because Cracknell uses the material in his major work Towards a New Relationship, published in 1986, "as evidence against exclusivist, non-dialogical Christianity".(10) This recent publication also offers an "extended exposition" of the theme of relationship, as developed by the BCC and put forward in Relationships with People of Other Faiths: Guidelines for Dialogue in Britain (1981, revised edition 1983).(11)

Towards a New Relationship tackles the question 'how are we to be faithful to Christ in a religiously plural world?' noting the intellectual, ethical and pastoral implications. In the Introduction Cracknell establishes his position: he is committed to inter-faith dialogue (NT support); he sees the concept of 'relationship' between believing people as fundamental (experience through BCC work); God's activity in the world is not exclusive to the Christian church (OT and NT support). The question which remains, as he sees it, is to do with the specific activity of God in Christ:

> "Without an assertion of once-and-for-allness and a declaration of its cosmic implications, the Christian faith must change both its name and nature." (12)

Cracknell takes on the spade-work of exposing the dilemmas and possibilities for Christians aware of religious pluralism from a Christian perspective:

> "Our participation as Christians in inter-faith encounter will depend upon an understanding of God's purposes which allows us to be both open and honest, vulnerable and yet committed, and, in the words of the Fourth Gospel, 'to do the truth' in our time." (13)

The process of moving "towards a new relationship" involves shedding some "entails" inherited from past theology, namely, the exclusiveness of the Church as the locus of salvation (extra ecclesiam nulla salus, Council of Florence 1438-35), the missionary background which denigrated other religions, and the cultural assumptions of the imperialist era.[(14)] (See Chapter III.1.) The openness to acknowledging "that goodness and grace, truth and sanctity are to be found in individuals and communities of other than Christian faith" is to be combined with the commitment to Christ.[(15)] Working from the basis of the biblical evidence which suggests that God has been at work in "various and diverse ways", Cracknell asks how this can be so in "the light of the Christian understanding of the uniqueness and finality of their Jesus Christ".

It is interesting that the area Cracknell first explores for an answer is eschatology. Unlike the missionaries of the past for whom "the only conceivable eschatology was the triumphalist picture of all the nations gathered in to the one fold",[(16)] Christians today face the continuing prospect of occupying one fold amongst others and are having to make theological sense of this. Herein lies Cracknell's preference for a pluralist eschatology, for which he looks to John Hick and Wilfred Cantwell Smith in their belief that in the eschaton Christians will be Christians, Jews still Jews, Buddhists still Buddhists, etc. and that this will be so because, as Hick puts it, 'God has many names' and Smith that the "cumulative religious traditions" share faith in a transcendence.[17] Cracknell chooses the work of Arnulf Camps, in whose writing he discerns "a greater sense than in either Hick or Smith that the future 'pluriformity' will somehow be related to the Christian tradition",[18] to move inwards, as it were, to the soteriological nature of the Incarnation. In this sphere Cracknell finds Eastern Orthodox and Catholic thought stimulating (for instance, Georges Khodr's writing on the 'economy' of the Son and the 'economy' of the Holy Spirit), but does not pursue it.[19] Instead he takes up the Anglican document Towards a Theology of Inter-Faith Dialogue (referred to on page 71) and its consideration of Logos Christology and makes this the basis for an inclusivist theology for religious pluralism.

Tackling the 'exclusivist' text "I am the Way, the Truth and the Life" (John 14.6), Cracknell tenaciously holds on to the soteriological validity of other faiths whilst maintaining that Christ is the Way, with a combination of humility ("Christians have always to realize that they have but the most rudimentary understanding of the cosmic significance of the Logos who was incarnate in Jesus of Nazareth"), and dogmatism ("other religious traditions ....., though unbeknown to them, ... are immediately and directly in relationship to the One who is 'the Supreme Dominating Way' in the whole tumultuous movement of the world in progress").[20]

As to the rest of the 'exclusive' statement "no one comes to the Father but by me", Cracknell provides a convincing argument with illustrations drawn from the Judaic, Sikh, Indian Bhakti and African traditional religions, of the non-uniqueness to Christianity of the concept of God as Father. In the Johannine Logos Christology he finds a basis for supporting the whole statement. The Logos, the Universal Word, plays a "central role" in both creation and redemption, his function is to "bring light and life to the world", he is "everywhere at work".[21]. The incarnation, resurrection and ascension of the Word affirms the original creative relationship of all human beings to God.[22]

> "It is therefore in my view not only perfectly proper but also quite essential to an adequate theological response to the discovery of 'truth', 'revelation', 'faith' and 'love' outside the Christian community to invoke the Logos doctrine, and in this way to speak of an inclusive Christology." (23)

There emerges from his substantial references to William Temple and John Hick affirmation of the wider working of God through the Eternal Logos than in Jesus of Nazareth; this would suggest that God works 'savingly' in relation to 'the world' through the Word and in relation to Christians through Jesus, if Cracknell did not subsequently stress the centrality of the birth, death and resurrection of Jesus as forming the essential link between God and humankind.[24]

The pluralist religious eschatological and inclusivist Christology outlined by Cracknell provides, he feels, a theological basis on which Christians may proceed in interfaith dialogue and encounter. The freedom of the 'new relationship' - of being able to recognise God's presence in people of other faiths - dictates the way Christians should behave in dialogue and Cracknell elaborates the four principles suggested by the WCC. It also offers the possibility of a 'new spirituality' and here the policy of "openness and commitment" plays a focal role, where theology takes second place to experience. Cracknell refers to Bede Griffiths and William Johnston who have shared the spirituality of Hindu and Buddhist communities, and to the process of "passing over and coming back" (using John S. Dunne's description referred to on p.106), to exploring the riches of meditation, and to the endorsement of the ideas of pilgrimage, provisionality and basic communities.

2. The Contribution of Wesley Ariarajah

In our consideration of overseas mission in the last chapter we noted the importance of the contributions by overseas Methodists to the understanding of inter-cultural theology as a significant factor in relations with people of other faiths. Wesley Ariarajah, an ordained minister of the Methodist Church of Sri Lanka and formerly lecturer in the History of Religions at the Theological College of Lanka, is now Director of the Subunit on Dialogue of the WCC with particular responsibility for Christian-Hindu/Buddhist relations. He is therefore ideally placed to comment on the theology of interfaith dialogue and encounter.

In The Bible and People of Other Faiths (1985) Ariarajah stresses the importance of taking an overall view of the teaching of the Bible which enables us to see from the Creation and the Universal Covenant, through to narratives of Jonah and Nineveh and Peter and Cornelius, that all people are children of God, that God has sovereignty over all creation and that all people stand in a directly accessible relation to God.[25] Furthermore, Ariarajah points out that Jesus himself lived a God-centred life and in the Synoptic accounts of his ministry he never called himself the Son of God. Paul, John and Peter all offer statements of faith because they express the significance held of their relationship to Jesus.[26]

> "The problem begins when we take these confessions in the language of faith and love and turn them into absolute truths. It becomes much more serious when we turn them into truths on the basis of which we begin to measure the truth or otherwise of other faith-claims." (27)

Jesus taught that God accepted people, that his love was unconditional and for Ariarajah the heart of the gospel message is self-giving and vulnerability.

> "If we cannot accept others as God's children until they believe as we do, then we do not act or speak from within the message of the gospel." (28)

Ariarajah strongly criticises the 'package' concept offered by some evangelists for several reasons: the statement that Jesus is the Messiah rests on a Jewish framework and is meaningless to Hindus with "4000 years of spiritual tradition in understanding the mystery of life and relation to God";[29] "The decisiveness of Christ must be a matter of experience and should never be the subject of preaching";[30] Jesus ministered within his own tradition and taught that repentance had to do with a radical renewal of the relationship with God and one's neighbours.[31]

The conclusion which Ariarajah draws from his understanding of the Bible - that God is the centre of the message - and from being a Christian in a Hindu and Buddhist community, leads him to argue for the recovery of a theocentric theology for interfaith dialogue.

> "To be a Christian is to show one's readiness to discern the world from the standpoint of faith in Jesus Christ. But this will be done in the perspective of a wider understanding of God's relationship with the world. It will certainly rule out at least the a priori assumption that what does not come as a result of faith in Jesus Christ cannot be of God." (32)

That Christology is a core issue of Christian relations with other faiths is recognized by Ariarajah, but it is relativized in its importance by acknowledging that much biblical Christology is the result of attempts by Paul to understand the significance of Jesus and his resurrection and interpret this in various cultural settings, whereas the Old Testament and the ministry of Jesus are predominantly concerned with God's relation to humanity.

> "It is the conscious or unconscious equation of Christian mission with God's mission that makes it impossible for Christians to relate to the signs of the kingdom which they discern outside the Christian community." (33)

3. Cracknell, Ariarajah and Wesley

Some observations may be made regarding the contributions of Cracknell and Ariarajah. It is not intended that a comparison should be made of the works referred to: the scope and range of Cracknell's Towards a New Relationship is wider. What is interesting in setting The Bible and People of Other Faiths alongside it is that we are made acutely aware that from

Ariarajah's position as a Christian in a more fully religiously plural society in which Christianity arrived later on the scene, concern is focused sharply on the essence of the Gospel. Mission is for Ariarajah a mode of living, a response of love and acceptance; mission is primarily a matter of response to life and therefore dialogue, not the proclamation of truth claims.

It becomes necessary at this point to note the use of the terms 'exclusivist', 'inclusivist' and 'pluralist' which have emerged in turning our attention to the theology of inter-faith dialogue. They have come to identify broad types of Christian theological response to the question of how Christianity stands in relation to other world religions. The works of two writers are commended for their thorough consideration of theological contributions in this field: No Other Name? (1985) by Paul Knitter and Theology and Religious Pluralism (1986) by Gavin D'Costa. Knitter's book follows a "textbook design" in reviewing the different Christian models for understanding and approaching other religions and summarises clearly the perspectives of many theologians. His categories are, somewhat misleadingly, labelled 'conservative Evangelical', 'mainline Protestant' and 'Catholic', but appear to correspond broadly with the more commonly employed terms. We will take D'Costa's concise definitions of the various Christian 'paradigms' as a working guide. 'Exclusivism' holds that other religions are marked by humankind's fundamental sinfulness and are therefore erroneous and Christ (or Christianity) offers the only valid path to salvation;[34] 'inclusivism' affirms the salvific presence of God in non-Christian religions while still maintaining that Christ is the definitive and authoritative revelation of God;[35] and 'pluralism' maintains that other religions are equally salvific paths to the one God and Christianity's claim that it is the only path (exclusivism) or the fulfilment of other faiths (inclusivism) should be rejected.[36] Cracknell's major concern is to outline an inclusivist Christology and Ariarajah's to urge a theocentric theology for interfaith dialogue.

Although both Cracknell and Ariarajah are Methodists, their thinking summarised above is chiefly identifiable as Protestant in their Scriptural orientation, and 'ecumenical' in appeal - as would be expected from two such committed ecumenists. However, Cracknell does assert that "I return again and again to my Methodist roots as I enter into interfaith dialogue[37] and "it is no surprise to me that so many of Mr. Wesley's contemporary preachers are caught up in this (new movement in inter-religious dialogue)",[38] and we proceed to follow up the references he makes to John Wesley's teaching. For Ariarajah's specifically Methodist insights into mission we shall examine a paper presented to the Seventh Oxford Institute of Methodist Theological Studies at Oxford in 1982.

Cracknell finds that Wesley was a man of his time, under pressure from the exponents of natural religion, and at one with Calvin and Luther on the point that "we had, by nature, no knowledge of God, no acquaintance with him" in his Sermon "Original Sin".[39] "In this Sermon", says Cracknell,

"Christianity stands or falls by the truth of its radical assessment of the desperate need of humanity for a Physician, a Healer of Souls". However, Cracknell detects an ambivalence in Wesley's opinion of humanity's fundamental sinful state and finds "a pervading awareness of natural theology" in several Sermons, such as the opening of "On Working Out Our Own Salvation":

> "Some great truths, as the being and attributes of God, and the difference between moral good and evil, were known in some measure, to the heathen world."(40)

Cracknell notes Martin Schmidt's comment that:

> "it would not be difficult to build up, by one-sided selection from his statements, a theologia naturalis of the heathen as a section of humanity pleasing to God".(41)

Wesley leaves to Him who is the "God of the Heathens as well as the Christians" the matter of final judgement on "the heathen and Mahometan world" in "On Living Without God".(42) Cracknell continues to deduce a positive attitude on the part of Wesley to God's final saving grace outside Christianity by quoting the following, which, incidentally, is from the Sermon "On Charity", and not, as Cracknell's passage suggests, from "On Living Without God":

> "True religion, in the very essence of it, is nothing short of holy tempers. Consequently all other religion whatever name it bears, whether Pagan, Mahometan, Jewish or Christian; whether Popish or Protestant, Lutheran or Reformed; without these is lighter than vanity itself."

Cracknell further draws attention to Wesley's admiration for the Muslim who wrote the Life of Hai Ebn Yokdan which "contains all the principles of pure religion and undefiled". The Sermon "On Faith" from which this is quoted is worthy of general attention according to Cracknell; he relates it to the work of

Wilfred Cantwell Smith on the world history of religions in which faith is seen as "the prodigious hallmark of being human".[43]

Cracknell closes this first chapter on "The Old Relationships" with a lengthy quotation of Wesley in his most scathing denunciation of Muslims ("as utter strangers to all true religion as their four-footed brethren" etc.), taken from the Sermon "The General Spread of the Gospel", to represent Wesley's "normal opinion" of the Muslim world. Cracknell concludes that it is necessary to free ourselves of the "entails" of our Christian tradition which are diversions away from more authentic understanding.

In his chapter "Towards a New Spirituality" Cracknell identifies the greatest Methodist stimulus for inter-faith encounter in Wesley's Sermon "The Catholic Spirit", in its "quite extraordinary openness to other traditions which marked the spirituality of the founder of Methodism".[44] The text is II Kings 10:15 and relates the meeting of Jehu with Jehonadab:

> "'Is your heart true to my heart as mine is to yours?' And Jehonadab answered, 'It is.' Jehu said, 'If it is, give me your hand'."

Cracknell appreciates Wesley's insight that people being what they are, men will differ in their opinions about religion as much as in other matters, but that this does not mean that they cannot love one another. He quotes Wesley's definition of catholic love, which is, that while a man is convinced of his own religious beliefs and the rightness of his way of worship and has special ties with his own congregation,

> "his heart is enlarged towards all mankind, those he knows and those he does not; he embraces with strong and cordial affection neighbours and strangers, friends and enemies." (45)

So in looking to his "Methodist roots" Cracknell says:

> "I, for one, have no doubt on the evidence that I presented in the first chapter that Wesley himself would have recognized faith and love and hope in the people that I have to deal with and would have walked the same way with us. What he wrote of the universal catholic love applying to all human beings is surely seminal, but like him, I also hold fast to what I know of Jesus. I am open to God at work everywhere but committed to Jesus through whom I know God." (46)

In his paper "Evangelism and Wesley's Catholicity of Grace" presented at the Seventh Oxford Institute of Methodist Theological Studies (1982), Ariarajah draws attention to the complex nature of evangelism and different understandings of it among Christians arising from various interpretations of the Scriptures and conditioning by the personal experience of both the mediators and the hearers of the 'good news'. Moreover, most importantly,

> "Evangelism happens, not when the evangelist's attentions are fulfilled, nor when persons cross from one commitment to another, but when God's intention is fulfilled in a given life or situation." (47)

It is with these factors in mind that Ariarajah examines Wesley's catholicity of grace, noting that:

> "his own evangelical experience was very much part of his own spiritual pilgrimage, which began under the wing of his mother, Susanna. His upbringing, his intense study of the Scriptures, the search for personal holiness, the experience of assurance commonly said to have been received at Aldersgate Street, and his quest for perfection, were all part of the pilgrimage." (48)

Like Cracknell, Ariarajah is conscious of the eighteenth

century context in which Wesley was operating and feels that Wesley faced the problem of the salvation/damnation of people of other faiths by not subscribing to the theory of "total depravity" like some of the Reformers, but believed that "God's law is written in the heart of every human being."[49] This was possible for Wesley because of the catholicity of his doctrine of grace.

> "He talked of grace in at least three aspects: prevenient (or preventing) grace, justifying grace and sanctifying grace. With the doctrine of prevenient grace, he was able to modify the extreme position that the "natural" human condition 'belongs to the devil'. He claimed that God's grace is already present and active in the natural person, moving and inviting towards saving grace, and commonly identified as conscience." (50)

The significance of this doctrine, as Ariarajah sees it, is firstly, that God's grace is available to all human beings, and secondly, the Christological, pneumatological dimensions "presuppose the Triune God of the Christian faith."

> "It is prevenient in the sense of 'before faith' and not 'before Christ'. He believed that through faith we move in freedom from prevenient grace to justifying and sanctifying grace." (51)

Referring to Works 7:188, Ariarajah draws attention to Wesley's belief that Christ works even in those who do not hear the gospel in this life, and are judged by their response to the universal grace and are justified by faith in anticipation of the full revelation of Christ. This insight is highly relevant to evangelism in a religiously plural world, concludes Ariarajah.

> "The evangelistic task is not to deny this universal grace, but to help persons move from 'grace to grace'. The theological task lies in trying to understand the nature of the relationship between this universal grace of God available to all and the salvation offered to humanity in the life, death and resurrection of Jesus Christ." (52)

Ariarajah stresses Wesley's wholistic approach to the individual (inward and outward holiness), to social and political living, and his universal eschatological vision, which never saw conversion as the only purpose of evangelism.(53)

In conclusion, Ariarajah argues that "while the Methodist traditions can, as we have observed, help us avoid some of the pitfalls of contemporary evangelism" Wesley was a man of his time and a significant feature of our time is that "we have entered a new era in our relationships with other religious traditions." Methodism must continue to be a "living tradition" responsive to the complexity of the contemporary world.

4. John Wesley and Encounter with Other Faiths

John Munsey Turner suggests that Wesley's theological stance could be set out as an "Epworth Triangle":

> "the priority of God's universal love; the need for a personal faith; no limitations can be put to God's grace in its effect on humanity given the limitations of living in a body in a fallen world." (54)

Turner is writing on Wesley's theology in the context of studies in Methodism and Ecumenism 1740-1982. We noted in Chapter III that the ecumenical movement has in significant respects been a necessary precursor to interfaith dialogue, and the "fresh look" at Methodist theology in the light of contemporary stimuli has highlighted the necessity for continuing the process of reassessing the dynamic of scripture, tradition, experience and reason (the "Wesley Quadrilateral") in response to the needs of the times. The fresh appraisal of Wesley's theology from an intra-faith perspective carries implications for inter-faith dialogue also - a fact which Turner acknowledges, even if he is not comfortable with the direction it seems to be taking. The outcomes of dialogue, as we noted in Chapter I, cannot be known!

In giving attention to "the priority of God's universal love" Turner points out Wesley's debt to the Arminian doctrine of universal grace and the free movement of the Spirit:(55)

> "Modern revivals of the idea of Christ, as the head of the whole human family, 'the light that lighteth every man' are not far from Wesley's position." (56)

Turner sees a danger in emphasising Wesley's view of an "optimism of grace", the "Arminianism of the heart":(57)

> "Now can this 'Arminianism of the heart' withstand the impact of the reality of God in other religions or the almost total eclipse of hell in the mainstream of Christian tradition? The first was just over Wesley's horizon ..... Hell - though never overstressed by Wesley - was part of the apparatus of the people's theologian. Perhaps at its lowest we can say that Wesley's point has been taken only too well and the danger now is of an uncritical universalism with judgement drained away." (58)

For Methodists like Cracknell and Ariarajah, for whom interfaith encounter and dialogue is a positive option, the "impact of the reality of God in other religions" is to be welcomed, rather than withstood.

The universal nature of God's love and the priority of His grace, then, are found to be sound starting points in Wesley for Cracknell and Ariarajah's inter-faith dialogue, and support Ariarajah's plea for a theocentric theology relating to people of other faiths; put in the simplest Biblical terms, "In the beginning, God". The danger of "judgement drained away" taken in relation to other religions requires further investigation. The issue of Christianity as one of the world religions was indeed "over Wesley's horizon" in the immediate sense in which it is to us today, but he was aware of the tension and was never one to avoid a debate.

> "But it may be asked, 'If there be no true love of our neighbour, but that which springs from the love of God; and if the love of God flows from no other fountain than faith in the Son of God; does it not follow, that the whole heathen world is excluded from all possibility of salvation?'"

Wesley's answer is unequivocal and, typically, scriptural:

> "I answer, St. Paul's words, spoken on another occasion, are applicable to this: 'What the law speaketh, it speaketh to them that are under the law'. Accordingly, that sentence, 'He that believeth not shall be damned', is spoken of them to whom the Gospel is preached. Others it does not concern; and we are not required to determine any thing touching on their final state. How it will please God, the Judge of all, to deal with <u>them</u>, we may leave to God himself. But this we know, that <u>he</u> is not the God of the Christians only, but the God of the Heathens also. ..... 'in every nation, he that feareth God and worketh righteousness is accepted of him'." ("On Charity")(59)

This understanding is not an incidental aside; Wesley returns to it in his Sermon "On Living Without God", (1790) to which Cracknell referred.[(60)]

Colin Williams is of the opinion that Wesley's doctrine of prevenient grace is Christocentric:

> "First it is his belief that Christ works even in those who do not hear the gospel in this life. Second, he believes that those who do not hear the gospel are judged according to their response to this grace by which Christ works within them in a hidden way. Finally there is a state of Paradise ..... in which a full knowledge of Christ is given and the souls of just men are made perfect." (61)

In keeping with this, Williams further refers to Wesley's view of the work of the Holy Spirit as Christocentric and quotes Wesley's note to John 15:26 (Explanatory Notes Upon the New Testament) as indicating "an orthodoxy which accepts the credal formulations, including the Western 'filioque' clause".(62)

> "The Christocentric nature of his work is made quite clear. His main task is to help us to receive Christ as Lord and to reveal to us the truth concerning Christ." (63)

It is at the point of justification, says Williams of Wesley's doctrine, "that the proper work of the Holy Spirit begins as it is here that the believer is born", rather than as the bearer of prevenient grace in which situation he works "in a hidden way".(64)

All Wesley's ministry, apart from the twenty-two months he spent in America (February 1736 - December 1737), was devoted to "stirring up" Britains to become holy - people who were 'nominal', lapsed, or 'almost' Christians. It is therefore quite in keeping with the context of his mission that Wesley should be primarily concerned with clarifying the work of the Holy Spirit in the lives of people in some way or another "under the Christian dispensation".

It is worthy of notice that the Explanatory Notes upon the New Testament from which Williams draws his conclusions on Wesley's view of the "Christocentric" nature of the work of the Spirit, refer to John's Gospel (14:26; 15:26; 16:8), I Corinthians (12:3) and I John (2:27). Where the Holy Spirit is mentioned in the Synoptics, Wesley's view is not Christocentric: for example, the note to Luke 1:35, in the account of the Annunciation, reads:

"'The Holy Ghost shall come upon thee, and the power of the Highest shall overshadow thee' - the power of God was put forth by the Holy Ghost, as the immediate divine agent in this work; and so he exerted the power of the Highest as His own power, who, together with the Father and the Son, is the Most High God."

On the occasion when "Jesus was led up by the Spirit into the wilderness" (Matthew 4:1), Wesley's explanation of 'by the Spirit' is "Probably through a strong inward impulse". In both these instances Wesley seems to view the Holy Spirit as having a dimension distinguishable from Jesus and which is not "sent" by him. On the text Luke 3:22 "the Holy Ghost descended in a bodily form as a dove upon him", Wesley is silent. In relation to the two occasions when Luke speaks of the Holy Ghost being upon other people, Zacharias and Simeon, (1:67; 2:25) Wesley makes no allusion to the Holy Ghost in the former and in the latter case says "'The Holy Ghost was upon him' - that is, he was a prophet".

Wesley's observation, then, of the working of the Holy Spirit is not exclusively confined to his procedure from the Son as well as the Father. While his Sermons on the Holy Spirit are mainly concerned with his work in the lives of committed or aspiring Christians, Wesley's only Sermon on the Trinity, written in 1775, on the text "There are three that bear witness in heaven, the Father, the Word and the Holy Ghost: and these three are one" (I John:7), is cautious: "I insist upon no explication at all; no, not even the best I ever saw". The manner of functioning of the Trinity is not a matter of belief, says Wesley, so opinions and explanations about this may legitimately vary[(65)] - a view which is shared today by Hans Küng, writing on Muslim-Christian dialogue.[(66)]

It is suggested in the light of current interest in the filioque clause in inter-faith dialogue (see for example the Church of England Document Towards a Theology for Inter-faith Dialogue, pages 20-21), that Wesley's "Christocentric" emphasis on the work of the Holy Spirit may be due in part to the necessities of the context of his own mission and that there are indications in his writings, such as those referred to above, which combine with his teaching on prevenient grace and belief in the universal grace of God to support what the Church of England document describes in the following way:

> "this vision of tension and complementarity between the historically visible, 'named', determinate presence and memory of God the Son and the more unpredictable, culturally and historically indeterminate witness of the spirit provides a possible fruitful vehicle for a 'theology of religions'." (67)

Wesley's statement of his universal mission is often quoted. The context, recorded in Wesley's Journal of 11th July 1739 was, in fact, ecclesiological; Wesley had been taken to task for assembling Christians who were not in his clerical charge and his response was:

> "I look upon all the world as my parish; thus far I mean, that, in whatever part of it I am, I judge it meet, right and my bounden duty, to declare unto all that are willing to hear, the glad tidings of salvation." (68)

In The Young Wesley Martin Schmidt underlines Wesley's self-identification with the heathen and quotes his Journal entry of 1st July 1736 relating his conversation with Tomochichi, chief of the Creek Indians, in Georgia:

> "If red men will learn the good book, they may know as much as the white men. But neither we nor you can understand that book, unless we are taught by Him that is above; and He will not teach, unless you avoid what you already know is not good." (69)

In his letter to John Burton explaining why he has decided to take up his suggestion to go to America, Wesley says that his "chief motive" is to save his own soul.[70] Schmidt strongly emphasises that the venture was necessary for Wesley because he believed it was the way in which he would, following the example of primitive Christians, grasp the meaning of the Gospel. However, Wesley's brief opportunities for mission to the heathen in America (the Indians, the Spanish-speaking Jews and the negroes in South Carolina), which his duties as parish priest to the English community allowed, present, in Schmidt's words "a tragic picture".[71] In his Journal of 7th October 1737, at the end of his stay in America, Wesley gives a "hard - and surely, on the whole, unjust - verdict" on the Indians, saying that he had "neither met nor heard of any Indian who had the least desire for genuine and continuous Christian instruction" and called them liars, thieves, hooligans, murderers, adulterers, idlers and sensualists.[72] But Schmidt also notes that when Wesley returned to his evangelical work in England: "he sometimes said of Christians that they were more savage than the most savage Indians he had encountered".[73]

What may be deduced from these insights into Wesley's encounter with other faiths? Firstly, he believed that all people had a God-given awareness of transcendence which proffered a discrimination of good and evil living. Secondly, he did not rank himself above non-Christians as a needy recipient of God's grace. Thirdly, he hoped that in preaching the gospel to the heathen in America, he would come to understand it himself.

What he came to understand, he recorded in his Journal after returning to England, was that he was "fallen short of the glory of God" and lacking in personal faith in Christ.[74] Much acknowledgement is given to the influence of the Moravians, the Herrnhut community and Peter Böhler for the part they played in Wesley's spiritual journey,[75] but little attention has been given until recently to the effect on Wesley of his encounter with other faiths in this respect, although it occurred in the same formative two years. James Fowler notes it in his paper "John Wesley's Development in Faith", presented to the 1982 Oxford Institute of Methodist Theological Studies. He writes:

> "the self-deception (or better, lack of self-knowledge) from which Wesley to this point had unknowingly suffered, was punctured in the events surrounding his abortive romance and failed mission to the Indians. ..... Georgia, for all its pain, was John Wesley's point of entry into a sense of real identification with the human race. It was to become a gateway to grace." (76)

A few months later, in May 1738, the reading of Luther's Preface to the Epistle to the Romans at a meeting in Aldersgate Street prompted the famous "conversion experience":

> "I felt I did trust in Christ, Christ alone for salvation. And an assurance was given me, that he had taken away <u>my</u> sins, even <u>mine</u>, and saved <u>me</u> from the law of sin and death." (78)

This, Turner's 'second side' of the 'Epworth Triangle', is the "Centrality of being put in right relationship with God by grace through faith".[82]

It is a fact that for the remaining fifty-three years of his life Wesley chose not to renew his personal mission to the American Indians, Jews or Negroes, or to initiate it with Hindus or Muslims. We are compelled to ask, in our current study of Methodist involvement with people of other faiths, why the great evangelist, for whom the most arduous and forbidding travels presented no obstacle, confined his mission to Britain and Ireland. He apparently never again felt called upon to evangelise amongst people of other religions, and as Schmidt points out in his theological biography of Wesley:

> "It was always a case of responding to an invitation, whether it came from a layman or a preacher ..... The opposite was also true. If there were no invitation from the field itself, even if the offer came from among his own circle, it was rejected. That happened on 14th February 1784, when at a conference of his preachers it was discussed whether anyone should be sent to the East Indies as a missionary." (79)

Birtwhistle is of the opinion that Wesley vetoed this latter enterprise - advocated by Thomas Coke in 1783 in his "Plan of the Society for the Establishment of Missions among the Heathens" - because a) the Society would have threatened Wesley's autonomy and b) he wanted Coke to found a church in America.[(80)] These may have been factors, but perhaps not so significant as the reason given in the Journal: "we have no call thither yet, no invitation, no providential opening of any kind".[(81)] This proposed mission was specifically to non-Christians in the British dominions in Asia, and we noted in Chapter III that the missionary response of Methodists had characteristically been to the call from ex-patriot communities abroad. It was not until 1786, just five years before Wesley died, that Conference, in Birtwhistle's words, "finally and formally shouldered its overseas missionary responsibility".[(82)] Wesley's mission, as we noted in our study of Ecumenism in Chapter III, was the evangelical revival of the Church of England. Schmidt summarises Wesley's view of the Methodists:

> "God has sent them to the lost sheep of the Church of

> England, and they are not the founders or leaders of a new sect; they are his messengers to those who bear the name of Christian but who in heart and life are heathens. Their task was to call those people back to that from which they had fallen, to real genuine Christianity." (83)

The outcome of Wesley's missionary encounter with people of other faiths, then, was an awareness of the inadequacy of his own faith and life - a factor contributing to his 'conversion' experience. The rest of his long ministry was devoted to people who regarded themselves as Christians and he felt other Methodists should do the same, unless specifically invited to do otherwise.

It is undoubtedly also true that Wesley had a vision of universal holiness and happiness (occurring in that order) which entailed the whole world becoming Christian. This is quite clear in his Sermon "The General Spread of the Gospel". This sermon envisaged the rapid and unstoppable spread of the "leaven of pure and undefiled religion, of the experimental knowledge and love of God, of inward and outward holiness" in "the dawn" of the "latter day glory"; the salvation of the world would proceed apace from the basis of what had already been begun fifty years previously with a group of young men in Oxford, the "small leaven", following the routes mapped out by colonial and trade expansion beyond the current bounds of Christendom.(84) Cracknell quoted from the sermon to illustrate Wesley's adverse criticism of Muslims (see page 126 above), but further reading puts these remarks in a different perspective, for it is but one part of a survey of the dreadful state of the world at the time, and no less harsh words are delivered on Christians:

> "Put Papists and Protestants, French and English together, the bulk of one and of the other nation; and what manner of Christians are they? Are they 'holy as He that hath called them is holy?' Are they filled with 'righteousness, and peace, and joy in the Holy Ghost?' Is there 'that mind in them which was also in Christ Jesus?' And do they 'walk as Christ walked?' Nay, they are as far from it as hell is from heaven!" (85)

Wesley is very clear that the spread of Christianity to all the inhabitants of the world rests not on proclamation and preaching, but on the way in which Christians live. The lives of Christians present "the grand stumbling block". Only when Christians "do the will of God on earth", being filled with the Holy Spirit, then:

> "the Mahometans will look upon them with other eyes, and begin to give attention to their words. And as their words will be clothed with divine energy, attended with the demonstration of the Spirit and of power, those of them that fear God will soon take knowledge of the Spirit whereby the Christians speak."
>
> "The poor American savage will no more ask, 'What are the Christians better than us?' - when they see their steady practice of universal temperance, and of justice, mercy, and truth." (86)

In his missionary sermon Wesley did not place making truth claims for Christianity above "walking as Christ walked". The salvation of the world is not impeded by the unholiness of people of other religions, but by the unholiness of Christians. This Sermon reflects in some measure the outcome of Wesley's own personal encounter with people of other religions in America - a more honest appraisal of his own faith and life. The Sermon serves also as a salutory warning for Christians engaged in interfaith dialogue against comparing the best aspects of Christianity with the worst of other faiths. Wesley never underrated the chasm between the ideal and the actual Christian practice of inward and outward holiness.

Neither did he lose confidence in the belief that the chasm could be bridged, and here we reach Turner's third side of the Epworth triangle: belief in the limitlessness of God's grace, which Turner sees expressed in Wesley's doctrine of Christian Perfection. The doctrine was explored in Chapter III.3; here we will remind ourselves with Wesley's own summary in A Plain Account of Christian Perfection (1767):

> "In one view it is purity of intention, dedicating all the life to God. It is the giving God all our heart; it is one desire and design ruling all our tempers. It is the devoting, not a part, but all our soul, body and substance to God. In another view, it is all the mind which was in Christ, enabling us to walk as Christ walked. It is the circumcision of the heart from all filthiness, all inward as well as outward pollution. It is a renewal of the heart in the whole image of God, the full likeness of Him that created it. In yet another, it is the loving God with all our heart, and our neighbour as ourselves." (87)

Wesley says "it is the doctrine of Jesus Christ" and here, in the very centre of the Christian life, is where the Methodist takes his/her vantage point for inter-faith encounter and dialogue in the light of Wesley's teaching on perfection. The doctrine is not "Jesus Christ", it is the doctrine *of* Jesus Christ: "Ye shall therefore be perfect, as your Father who is in heaven is perfect" (Matthew 5:48). Wesley's Explanatory Note reads:

> "referring to all that holiness which is described in the foregoing verses, which our Lord at the beginning of the Chapter recommends as happiness, and in the close of it as perfection. ..... And how wise and gracious is this, to sum up, and as it were seal, all His commandments with a promise, ... (Jesus) stakes upon it all the power, truth and faithfulness of Him to whom all things are possible."

To "walk as Christ walked" is to wholly love God and people, to renew the created likeness to God. For Wesley, living in right relationship with God and humanity was primarily a matter of following the example of Jesus in these respects. Cracknell, we noted above (page 127), says in relation to Wesley: "like him I also hold fast to what I know of Jesus. I am open to God at work everywhere **but** committed to Jesus through whom I know God". (Emphasis added) Being 'committed to Jesus' could be interpreted as an end in itself, whereas what Jesus taught, and what Wesley grasped in his understanding of perfect love, was that this commitment is the beginning of a qualitatively different relationship to God and other people. Loyalty to Jesus can only be because of what he, as a man, illuminates - God beyond, God within and God-in-relation to the world - by his life, death and resurrection. The personal life-transforming relationship to Jesus often stressed by Methodists is not a final objective but a means ("Way") of nurturing a radical relationship with God and other members of humanity, (or as Wesley would put it, inward and outward holiness). Weatherhead, for whom we saw earlier, the presence of God was realised through his friendship with Jesus, says, reflecting on the crucifixion:

> "the friendship of Jesus, as it meets the test of the Cross, shows the nature of the friendship also of God Himself. Here is a love revealed to our wondering eyes which, long before Christ came, was loving and suffering for men in a manner which only Christ could reveal, and which will go on loving and suffering until the last soul is voluntarily brought into harmony with Himself in the final perfection of the ultimate heaven." (88)

The theocentric/christocentric issue is important for Methodists entering relationships with people of other faiths, not least because it obliges each one to re-examine their understanding of Christ.

Whilst Wesley's Sermons and Journal were written for public

consumption, some letters to his brother Charles were clearly private, and to such an end, scattered with Greek and his own personal form of shorthand. One of these letters, written at Whitehaven on June 27th 1766 reinforces observations we have made in our foregoing examination of Wesley's understanding of mission. Schmidt comments that: "for Wesley missions signify an existential task, to be taken up with fervour from inner necessity"[89], and we recall Ariarajah's observation that Wesley's "evangelical experience was very much part of his own spiritual pilgrimage" (see page 127). In this letter we see in his 'thinking aloud' to Charles that creative tension of humility and doubt, commitment and vocation which we glimpsed in his encounter with other faiths but which, at that point in his journey he articulated in different terms. The words in brackets in the following extract were originally 'in code'.

> "(I do not love God. I never did). Therefore (I never) believed in the Christian sense of the word. Therefore (I am only an) honest heathen, a proselyte of the Temple, one of the φοβουμένοι τὸν Θεόν.[1] And yet to be so employed of God! and so hedged in that I can neither get forward or backward! ..... (I have no) direct witness, I do not say that (I am a child of God), but of anything invisible or eternal.
>
> And yet I dare not preach otherwise than I do, either concerning faith, or love, or justification, or perfection. And yet I find rather an increase than a decrease of zeal for the whole work of God and every part of it. I am φερόμενος,[2] I know not how, that I can't stand still. I want all the world to come to ὃν οὐκ οἶδα[3]. Neither am I impelled to this by fear of any kind. I have no more fear than love. Or if I have (any fear, it is not that of falling) into hell but of falling into nothing."
>
> 1 'Those that fear God'; 2 'Borne along';
> 3 'What I do not know'. (90)

"I am only an honest heathen" - perhaps the contemporary Methodist's pilgrimage amongst people of other faiths demands also reaching a point of abandonment, of fully "identifying with the human race" (Fowler, page 136 above) and having the courage to move.

John S. Dunne describes the "passing over" to other faiths in this way:

> "Passing over to other men, entering into their lives by sympathetic understanding, is an experience of sympathy and resonance. It means finding within yourself something corresponding to what you see in another." (91)

He says this is a standpoint of "universal compassion. It is really a divine standpoint"; it is a "passing over to God".[92] In "coming back" we see our own concreteness and individuality as richer.[93] There is something here also of Wesley's "Catholic Spirit": this sermon took as its inspiration the unlikely text of the crossing of ways of a Rechabite and an idol-worshipper (see pages 126-127 above). Wesley applies this striking 'meeting of hearts' to the nature of a loving relationship between two Christians: is it such a big step for the contemporary Methodist to enter such a relationship with a Buddhist, Sikh, Jew, Hindu or Muslim? And is this Wesley's "universal love"?

Before leaving Wesley, two general observations may be made. Firstly, Albert Outler enthusiastically points out that there is "a sort of catalytic theology" in Wesley, "designed to interact with other theologies (earlier and later) without losing its own integrity, and without forcing Christian doctrines into a rigid mold".[94] This is a talent to be usefully emulated. It is not necessary (or desirable) to attribute to Wesley the "openness" to the beliefs and opinions of other religions which he most certainly extended to other Christian traditions.[95] This was, indeed, "over his horizon". We can look to his movement around the 'quadrangle' of scripture, tradition, experience and reason with confidence as a continuing guide to interpreting the place of Christianity in our contemporary world situation. Secondly, Turner says of Wesley that:

> "he worked out his theology not so much in the 'groves of academe' but on horseback and in dialogue with friend and foe." (96)

We do not need the horse.

5. Observations

That Methodist theology is developed from personal experience is reflected in the thinking of the men whose work we have considered. Cracknell respects the people of other faiths with whom his work has brought him into contact and recognises the presence of God in their midst; Ariarajah cannot love his Buddhist and Hindu neighbours less because they are not Christian. Wesley shatters illusions about the superiority of Christians: he did not take as his life's mission the conversion of people of other faiths to Christianity; he did not consider people of other faiths condemned to hell; he saw God as being in creative and gracious relationship to all humanity; he viewed holiness as an individual pilgrimage with universal implications, and defined it, for Christians, in terms of love - the response of faith to the God of Love made known to them through Jesus, and which results in action (works). Wesley says that we do not know all there is to know,

"But, if we die without love, what will knowledge avail?"(97)

It follows from this that Methodist encounter and dialogue with people of other faiths is not about making claims for possession of 'the truth', it is not about adding numbers to the Church, it is not about 'reaching the parts God cannot reach' (for there are none), it is not about eschatological judgements on other people (they are not ours to make). It is simply participating in the life of the world as a person-in-relation-to-Christ, being willing to enter understanding, sympathetic, self-sacrificing relationships with our neighbours, "to walk as Christ walked", and through this maturational experience of loving relationship in which God, our neighbour and ourselves are revealed, to be led to 'the truth'.

> "If we believe that the Spirit of Truth is always guiding us into the truth, we shall see clearly that he who is not willing to move cannot be guided anywhere." (98)

6. Willing to Move: Two Methodist Examples

Geoffrey Parrinder, a Methodist minister, spent twenty years teaching in his native West Africa and studying African religions. He subsequently became Professor of the Comparative Study of Religions in the University of London and in 1964 had published The Christian Debate: Light from the East, a response to John Robinson's Honest to God and the ensuing heated controversy. Parrinder wrote:

> "the bishop may be right in denouncing outworn language and ideas that were formulated by Jews over two thousand years ago or Greek theologians in the early Christian centuries. But these are not the only ways of

> understanding the universe that religious thinkers have discovered during the history of humanity."

He continued:

> Instead of the religions of the West thinking they should fight those of the East, they might consider whether they have not unexpected allies in the East, and whether it is not a matter of concern to us all to appreciate each other's searches after truth". (99)

It is his conviction that religious education is needed in every generation and that today it should also include the study of religions other than Christianity. In What World Religions Teach, whilst stressing the importance of laying strong foundations of Christian teaching he makes the point:

> "to study other religions, at higher school and university level, is not to discredit Christianity. It is to seek a wider understanding of the religious experiences of mankind, to recognize that God has never left himself without witness, and to appreciate the workings of the divine Spirit at many times and in different manners." (100)

Writing in 1965, he describes the time as "for ploughing, not reaping", as a time of acquiring the knowledge of other religions and their scriptures now generally available. Parrinder identifies the pastoral need as well as the theological need to include "these new worlds of thought and apprehensions". "Ordinary" people, when confused, turn to their ministers before they look to leading Christian thinkers - ministers therefore need educating in more than just comparative religion.[101]

A quarter of a century later we must ask to what extent we have availed ourselves of all this information on our neighbours' religions. Have we educated ourselves, "ploughed" in preparation for the sowing of new thinking? And how are we educating the next generation for life in a plural, but common world? Ninian Smart writes on this issue (1987):

> "our children are entering into a new global civilization: the standards of the 1950's are not good enough to cope with their future. I would consider cultural tribalism always to be wrong: but it is especially egregrious when we now live in a global civilization." (102)

Three important strands may be identified in Parrinder's strategy: firstly, it is necessary to know something about other religions' teachings and ways of worship; for this, commitment to Christianity is an asset, not an obstacle:

> "a believer does not try to explain away the existence of a great religion, like Islam or Hinduism, he seeks to understand its strength and appeal because he knows the value of religion to his own life." (103)

Secondly, and dependent on this preliminary education, similarities and differences can be noted, and mutual enrichment becomes possible:

> "Christians today can learn from other religions, in meditation, tolerance, and peace. Christianity offers a faith of love and service to humanity, which is what modern man needs, and is as necessary today as it ever has been." (104)

Thirdly, the field of world religions and their relationship to each other can and should be extended beyond academic specialists to "ordinary" people. The style and format of Parrinder's many books bear testimony to this.

Another overseas Methodist, Lynn de Silva, was also 'willing to move'. De Silva also believed in "ploughing". Ordained into the Methodist Ministry in Sri Lanka in 1950, he pursued theological studies to doctoral level and was equally committed to studying Buddhism. He published a book in 1974 entitled Buddhism: Beliefs and Practices in Sri Lanka. Buddhism had usually been presented as an intellectual philosophy but de Silva found it also to have "a religious sap which has made it a living vital religion" and explored the traditions, ceremonies, rites, rituals and myths "which have combined to form the faith by which these Buddhists live".(105) In 1975 this was followed by The Problem of Self in Buddhism and Christianity.

De Silva had been released from circuit ministry in 1962 to become Director of the Study Centre in Colombo (now the Ecumenical Institute for Study and Dialogue) and to continue Bible translation work (into Sinhala). In 1969 he became a member of the Committee of the Sub-unit on Dialogue of the WCC.

Aloysius Pieris, SJ, makes a pertinent observation in a Tribute to Lynn de Silva, after his death in 1982:

> "the preoccupation with the reconstruction of a theology which is contextually relevant to a Buddhist milieu remained paramount among his priorities even during his last days. It seems to me, however, that the subsequent exposure to the powerful message of the Buddha changed his perception of his own mission. There was over the years, a marked shift from the polemical to the ecumenical approach, from debate to dialogue." (106)

Pieris, who worked with de Silva for fifteen years, says of him:

> "The Christ he believed in was not dismembered by denominational divisions nor by ethnocentrism as was evident in the way he spoke and acted during the racial riots of 1977. The Ecumenical Institute was built on that belief. This also accounted for the spirit of freedom generated in his company." (107)

In a 1977 edition of Dialogue, the journal published by the Institute, concern was focused on inter-racial relationships in Sri Lanka. De Silva refers to the meetings and consultations in which Buddhists, Hindus, Muslims and Christians participated - "a significant happening", and to a programme initiated by the Institute to study the matter. He wrote:

> "people of all faiths have a vital role to play in bringing about racial harmony, since it is acknowledged that the Government alone cannot achieve this end by legislation and other measures." (108)

Lynn de Silva was a pioneer in Buddhist-Christian dialogue, and has not been without critics from both sides; his 'translational theology' continues to be assessed. What cannot be disputed is that he set an example in that his life, as a Christian, consisted in intra-faith and inter-faith encounter and dialogue. Brian de Alwis writes:

> "His holistic view of dialogue is the result of an awareness that comes from living in day-to-day contact with other religions, and sharply contrasts with the Western emphasis on an almost exclusively discursive dialogue. There is not only a meeting of minds at the intellectual level and a meeting of hearts for spiritual enrichment. De Silva also includes the 'socio-political level' with its emphasis that the solution of pressing social issues must be accomplished by dialogue between men of various faiths." (109)

Without exception, the Methodist theologies which we have considered in this chapter attest the centrality of relation, encounter and change as a Christian response to life. Openness and commitment are not seen by the Methodists we have considered as mutually exclusive attitudes, but as interdependent. None of them claim to possess all of the Truth or to have 'arrived'. Ariarajah puts it thus:

> "Commitment has no limiting boundaries: it has only roots. The deeper the roots the more the freedom to spread and to grow without being blown over." (110)

-oOo-

References

(1) Kenneth Cracknell, Why Dialogue?, p.6.

(2) Ibid, p.7.

(3) Ibid, pp.8-9.

(4) Ibid, p.10.

(5) Ibid, p.13.

(6) Ibid, p.13.

(7) Ibid, p.35; Cracknell here uses Jean Daniélou's phrase.

(8) Ibid, p.15.

(9) Gen 14:18; Gen 20:4; Exodus 18; Numbers 22-4; I Kings 17; 2 Kings 5; Ezekiel 14:14; Job 38.

(10) Kenneth Cracknell, Towards a New Relationship, p.5.

(11) Ibid, p.3.

(12) Ibid, p.5.

(13) Ibid, p.110.

(14) Ibid, Chapter 1, pp.8-24.

(15) Ibid, pp.6.

(16) Ibid, p.52.

(17) Ibid, pp.53-59.

(18) Ibid, p.60.

(19) Ibid, p.64.

(20) Ibid, p.79.

(21) Ibid, pp.98-117.

(22) Ibid, pp.106-107.

(23) *Ibid*, p.100.

(24) *Ibid*, p.107.

(25) Wesley Ariarajah, *The Bible and People of Other Faiths*, Chapters 1 and 2.

(26) *Ibid*, p.23.

(27) *Ibid*, p.26.

(28) *Ibid*, p.32.

(29) *Ibid*, p.55.

(30) *Ibid*, p.53.

(31) *Ibid*, p.50.

(32) *Ibid*, p.66.

(33) *Ibid*, p.70.

(34) Gavin D'Costa, *Theology and Religious Pluralism*, p.52.

(35) *Ibid*, p.80.

(36) *Ibid*, p.22.

(37) Kenneth Cracknell, *Towards a New Relationship*, p.133.

(38) *Ibid*, p.57.

(39) *Ibid*, p.12.

(40) *Ibid*, p.14.

(41) *Ibid*, p.13, referring to Martin Schmidt, *The Young Wesley: Missionary and Theologian of Missions*, Epworth Press, 1958.

(42) *Ibid*, p.14.

(43) *Ibid*, pp.56, 15..

(44) *Ibid*, p.131.

(45) *Ibid*, p.132.

(46) *Ibid*, p.133.

(47) Wesley Ariarajah, "Evangelism and Wesley's Catholicity of Grace", in *The Future of the Methodist Theological Traditions*, p.140.

(48) *Ibid*, p.141.

(49) *Ibid*, p.142.

(50) *Ibid*, pp.142-3.

(51) Ibid, p.143.

(52) Ibid, p.144.

(53) Ibid, p.146.

(54) John Munsey Turner, Conflict and Reconciliation: Studies in Methodist Ecumenism 1740-1982, p.45.

(55) Ibid, p.46. Turner writes, referring to the Four Articles of the Remonstrance of 1605 in H. Bettenson, Documents of the Christian Church, pp.268-9: "Arminius stated that the atonement was intended to be available for all, that people are incapable of saving faith without the Holy Spirit, that divine grace is indispensable for salvation but not irresistible and that it is not certain that all believers will persevere to the end. Mankind is dependent on grace, yet is still free."

(56) Ibid, p.46.

(57) Ibid; the phrase is G. F. Nuttal's.

(58) Ibid, p.147.

(59) Sermons Vol.3, XCI "On Charity", p.45.

(60) "... nor do I conceive that any man living has a right to sentence all the heathen and Mahometan world to damnation. It is far better to leave them to Him that made them, and who is 'the Father of the spirits of all flesh'; who is the God of the Heathens as well as the Christians, and who hateth nothing that he hath made." Sermons Vol.3, CXXV "On Living Without God", p.337.

(61) Colin Williams, John Wesley's Theology Today, p.45.

(62) Ibid, p.98.

(63) Ibid, pp.98-99.

(64) Ibid, p.99.

(65) Sermons Vol.2, LV "On the Trinity", pp.187, 191.

(66) Hans Küng, Christianity and the World Religions, pp.121-122.

(67) Board for Mission and Unity of the Church of England, Towards a Theology for Inter-Faith Dialogue, pp.20-21.

(68) The Journal of John Wesley: A Selection, Editor Elisabeth Jay, p.44.

(69) Martin Schmidt, The Young Wesley, p.33.

(70) Ibid, Appendix II, pp.44-8.

(71) Ibid, p.40.

(72) Ibid, p.39.

(73) Martin Schmidt, John Wesley: a Theological Biography, Vol. 2, part 1, p.42.

(74) The Journal of John Wesley: a Selection, pp.25-6: the entry for February 1738, having arrived back from Savannah in December 1737.

(75) See, for example, Stanley Ayling, op. cit., Chapters IV and V.

(76) James Fowler, "John Wesley's Development in Faith", in The Future of the Methodist Theological Traditions, p.186.

(77) The Journal of John Wesley: A Selection, p.35: entry May 1738.

(78) John Munsey Turner, op. cit., p.48.

(79) Martin Schmidt, John Wesley: A Theological Biography, Volume 2, Part 1, p.94.

(80) N. Allen Birtwhistle, "Methodist Missions 1786-1838", in A History of the Methodist Church in Great Britain, Vol.3, pp.3-4.

(81) The Journal of John Wesley: a Selection, p.226.

(82) N. Allen Birtwistle, op. cit., p.7.

(83) Martin Schmidt, John Wesley: a Theological Biography, Vol.2, Part 1, p.148.

(84) Sermons Vol.2, LXIII "The General Spread of the Gospel", pp.263-265.

(85) Ibid, p.262.

(86) Ibid, p.268.

(87) John Wesley, "A Plain Account of Christian Perfection", Works X1:444.

(88) Leslie Weatherhead, The Transforming Friendship, p.158.

(89) Martin Schmidt, The Young Wesley, p.25.

(90) The Letters of John Wesley, Vol.V, pp.15-16.

(91) John S. Dunne, The Way of All the Earth, p.219.

(92) Ibid, p.220.

(93) Ibid, pp.220-221.

(94) Albert Outler, in The Future of the Methodist Theological Traditions, Ed. Douglas Meeks, p.44.

(95) This is particularly clearly stated in the Sermon "The Catholic Spirit", which Cracknell drew attention to. In the Sermon "A Caution against Bigotry" Wesley is explicit about his rationale for this toleration of differences of opinion among Christians and the overriding importance of love. Writing of the apostles (and forshadowing James Dunn by two hundred years) he says: "We do not find that even those pillars in the temple of God, so long as they remained upon the earth, were ever brought to think alike, to be of one mind, particularly with regard to the ceremonial law. It is therefore in no way surprising, that infinite varieties of opinion should now be found in the Christian church." (John Wesley's Forty-Four Sermons, pp.434-435.)

(96) John Munsey Turner, Conflict and Reconciliation, p.44.

(97) John Wesley's Forty-Four Sermons, Preface, p.vii.

(98) Leslie Weatherhead, The Christian Agnostic, p.31.

(99) Geoffrey Parrinder, The Christian Debate: Light from the East, pp.11,12.

(100) Geoffrey Parrinder, What World Religions Teach, Introduction to the 2nd Edition, p.9.

(101) Geoffrey Parrinder, Jesus in the Qur'an, pp.14-15.

(102) Ninian Smart, Religion and the Western Mind, p.7.

(103) Geoffrey Parrinder, What World Religions Teach, p.213.

(104) Ibid, p.214.

(105) Lynn de Silva, Buddhism: Beliefs and Practices in Sri Lanka, p.i.

(106) Aloysius Pieris, SJ, "Rev. Dr. Lynn A. De Silva: A Tribute"; Supplement to Dialogue Vol.9, 1-3 Jan-Dec 1982, p.3.

(107) Ibid, p.4.

(108) Lynn de Silva, Dialogue, Vol.IV No.3, Sep-Dec 1977, p.79.

(109) T. Brian de Alwis, "Christian Buddhist Dialogue in the Writings of Lynn A. De Silva"; Dialogue, Vol.X No.1, Jan-May 1983, p.34.

(110) Wesley Ariarajah, "The understanding and practice of dialogue: its nature, purpose and variations", in Faith in the Midst of Faiths, WCC, ed. Samartha, p.56.

CONCLUSION

Interfaith encounter and dialogue is not, as we concluded from our examination of a community in Birmingham and the attention given to the matter in the church structure, an irrelevance for Methodists. It does, however, present problems for many - from Pew to Conference. When we considered our contemporary situation and the scriptures we found that relation, dialogue and change are the means of response to life and our understanding of it. The history of Israel's encounter with God, the life and ministry of Jesus, and the growth of the early church all rest on this process. Yet there would seem to be considerable resistance to participation in dialogue - either passive, in terms of an uneasy truce, or active in terms of warnings against compromise, syncretism and unfaithfulness to 'the gospel'.

Difficulty seems to lie in our understanding of mission; terminology has changed over the years (evangelism, mission, service, witness) without clarification or definition. Attitudes to people of other colours, cultures and faiths are similarly ambiguous; this was reflected clearly in the views of lay Methodists. The problem of 'otherness' extends to other Christian traditions and, indeed, to fellow members of the same community. It was ever thus![(1)] 'What is my function?' cannot be answered without considering 'What is the nature of my relationship to?' These questions have constantly to be asked afresh. The attitudes of the church to people of other faiths in the nineteenth and early twentieth century era of colonialism - all too often those of triumphalism, superiority or patronage - are untenable in the light of contemporary realities: Christians remain a minority in the world, western Christian culture has not produced the Messianic Age but, in this century alone, two world wars, permanent threat of a nuclear holocaust, rapid pollution of the Earth and widespread starvation.

That reassessment and change are necessary, is, we noted, recognised through the Divisions and Connexional committees of the Methodist Church. What there is no consensus on, however, is what direction the change should take, and there is a danger of entrenchment in what Alistair Hunter describes as antagonistic positions between 'conservative evangelicals' and Christians who are forming bonds with believers of other faiths.[2] This is evident already in the marked tendency for people addressing the whole issue of Christianity's relation to other faiths to declare themselves as 'exclusivist', 'inclusivist' or 'pluralist' (or somewhere in between!). Whilst this conceptual framework has been immensely helpful in identifying and stimulating discussion on crucial areas, it is important to remember that categorisation can be limiting and restrictive.

Dialogue is a dynamic process; we observed in the biblical study of Chapter I that the outcomes of dialogue cannot be known and that the process is itself revelatory. In asking whether Methodists should welcome dialogue with people of other faiths we have explored something of our origin, history, theology and present position - poised at the open doorway. Such self appraisal is, it is believed, a necessary precursor to any ensuing dialogue with people of other religions; a clearer understanding of our own faith tradition and an acknowledgement that that understanding is always provisional, incomplete and open to new insight, is vital, not only to the functioning of the church, but also to the individual pilgrimage.

The experience and theological reflection of overseas Christians on relations with people of other faiths is seen as a valuable and developing resource for British Methodists. We have noted the contributions of Lynn de Silva, Geoffrey Parrinder and Wesley Ariarajah. S. Israel, a Presbyter of the Church of South India (of which what was Methodism now forms a part) and Lecturer in Religions at the Tamil Nadu Theological Seminary in Madurai, comments in an article on conversion in dialogue, "It is in the dialogical experience one can find how distorted the Christian gospel is as it is presented to the Hindus."(3) In criticising fundamentalist, evangelical, revivalist approaches on the part of the churches, he asks,

> "Is it not a shame for those, who themselves are not open for any change within their own tradition, to call the Hindus and Muslims to a conversion which would involve much greater sacrifice? The Bible not only demands a new orientation of life from all people but also speaks about the continued conversion of the church." (4)

We ignore at our peril the responses now coming from the old mission fields. Methodism, to its credit, developed the policy relatively early in its overseas missions of training and ordaining the indigenous people. It is to be hoped that we are prepared to learn from them.

British Methodism has shown itself to be willing to dialogue with other Christian traditions - and John Wesley is a shining light in this respect; if it is also willing to be renewed through dialogue within its own tradition, and through dialogue with overseas Methodists, then dialogue with people of other faiths becomes simply an extension of the same process. Jesus does not belong to the church; he was a Jew - have we nothing to learn from Judaism about him? And if we listen to what Judaism has to tell us about him, may our clarified understanding not help us to share what he means to us? In Jesus the Jew Geza Vermes quotes Martin Buber:

> "I am more than ever certain that a great place belongs to (Jesus) in Israel's history of faith ..... There is something in Israel's history of faith which is only to be understood from Israel." (5)

Similarly, if we are to reflect on Jesus in the framework of a Logos Christology for interfaith dialogue, as Cracknell suggests, then we should surely receive guidance from the Jewish Wisdom writings of Proverbs and Ecclesiasticus, as understood by Jews.(6) This is a dialogical process without proselytising but with the prospect of conversion - for all involved.

If we are willing to be a little more adventurous in risking our understanding of the gospel then we are fortunate in having an increasing number of individuals who have lived and studied within two faith communities and pioneered sympathetic and discriminating approaches to the interpretation of religions in relation to each other. One such is Dr. Antony Fernando, a Roman Catholic Sri Lankan married to a Buddhist, who has doctorates in Theology and in Buddhist studies. In his book Buddhism and Christianity: their inner affinity he makes a comparative study of the teachings of the Buddha and Christ and finds within their differences in teaching on the process of "personality transformation", that:

> "for both, the ultimate target of religion and religious liberation was one: the development of the person in man. For neither of them was religion, as it is for many today, just a matter of fidelity to religious practices or traditions. Nor was it for them just a matter of a happy life after death. For both of them, the field of operation too was exactly the same: the mind of man. It was the mind of man that was sick. It was the mind of man that had to be cured." (7)

Dr. Fernando is developing his "religiological" approach to the study of world religions, which is non-theological, by viewing religion as "the aspiration of human beings to be truly human", to perceive life as having a dimension beyond the personal satisfaction of the senses which extends from self-centredness to an outward-looking responsive and responsible attitude to the life of the universe. In every religion, he feels, there is the vision of a fruitful life, though different versions of what it is to be truly human and different paths to achieving it. If we start from the "common sense" approach of what it means to be a religious human being, then we can constructively explore the insights of different religions, and our own.[8] Such an approach could help Methodists pass freely back and forth through the open doorway, giving and receiving, maturing in Christian faith and experience, reflecting on and integrating new understanding.

John Wesley directs us to the perfection of love in individual Christians. Learning the meaning of love is a personal privilege and responsibility and no line is drawn between those with whom we should enter such a relationship and those we should not. Love, as Wesley describes it, especially in "The Catholic Spirit", is not simply courtesy, or kindness, or not doing any harm, any more than it is agreement on doctrine, belief, or worship: it is more strenuous, painful and demanding. Love - if we are to "have the mind that was in Christ" and "to walk as Christ walked" - hurts.

Interfaith encounter and dialogue, then, should and could be a positive option for Methodists, given the experience and breadth of their tradition and its emphasis on the nurturing and development of Christian Perfection. The theological reflection with which we concluded our study of Methodism and relations with people of other faiths is but a stage in the ongoing process of understanding the relationship between God, ourselves, other people and the world in which we live, part of "the great adventure of love".(9) We conclude with words of Leslie Weatherhead, a Methodist who exemplifies that it is possible to be both open and committed, and that it is possible to catch a glimpse of the immense and unconfined reality of the present and prospect for the future:

> "Christianity is a love relationship with Christ far below - or above, if you like - differences of belief or different ways of worshipping, far above differences of language or of colour. The Christianity of tomorrow will embrace all truth wherever it is found or however men have come to apprehend it, whether through specifically Christian teaching or through Buddhism or Mohammedanism, Hinduism, Confucianism, Taoism, Zoroastrianism or even through the bleak desert of apparent atheism. Many of our

greatest minds pass through the latter, feeling that to deny all is nearer the truth than to be identified with those who deny all approaches to truth save their own, and in their narrowness and exclusiveness deny love which is more fundamental than anything else." (10)

-oOo-

References

(1) See, for example, Walter Hollenweger, Conflict in Corinth.

(2) Alistair G. Hunter, Christianity and Other Faiths in Britain, p.122.

(3) S. Israel, "Religious conversion and Interfaith Dialogue" in Discernment, Vol.3, No. 2., Autumn 1989, p.8.

(4) Ibid, p.9.

(5) Geza Vermes, Jesus the Jew, p.223.

(6) Alistair Hunter, op. cit., pp.41-46.

(7) Antony Fernando, Buddhism and Christianity: their inner affinity, p.126.

(8) Antony Fernando, Lecture given at the Multi Faith Centre, Birmingham, 22.2.88.

(9) Michel Quoist, "I would like to rise very high", Prayers of Life, p.12.

(10) Leslie Weatherhead, The Christian Agnostic, p.4.

APPENDIX A

THE QUESTIONNAIRE

Schedule Number

Date Length of interview

Place of interview

INTRODUCTION

The purpose of the study is to find out how members of a Christian community describe and understand their relation to members of non-Christian religious communities (Hindus, Buddhists, Sikhs, Jews, Muslims).

1. MALE	2. AGE	14 - 18	3. LIVING ALONE
		19 - 25	
		26 - 35	LIVING WITH PARTNER
FEMALE		36 - 45	
		46 - 55	LIVING WITH OTHER ADULT(S)
		56 - 65	
		66 - 75	LIVING WITH CHILDREN
		76 or over	
			LIVING WITH PARENT(S)

4. OCCUPATION

PAID EMPLOYMENT

.... P/T F/T

OUTSIDE HOMEWORKER

SELF EMPLOYED

HOMEMAKER

SEEKING PAID EMPLOYMENT RETIRED

FORMER OCCUPATION

FULL TIME EDUCATION

5. RESIDENCE

DO YOU LIVE NEAR THE CHURCH? (Within a mile) YES NO

HOW LONG HAVE YOU LIVED THERE? ....

ARE YOU THINKING OF MOVING? YES NO

IF YES, FOR WHAT REASONS? ....

....

6a. DO YOU HOLD ANY OFFICES OR DO ANY JOBS IN THE CHURCH?

STEWARD | COMMUNION STEWARD

DOOR STEWARD | CRADLE ROLL SECRETARY

CHOIR | UNIFORMED ORGANISATIONS

MEMBER OF A COMMITTEE:

Church Council
Church Family
Finance
Pastoral
Womens Network

Home Missions
World Mission & Service
Neighbourhood
Worship Consultation

PASTORAL VISITOR | FLOWERS

PLAYGROUP LEADER | MOTHER & TODDLER LEADER

CLEANING | JUNIOR CHURCH

YOUTH CLUB | LUNCH CLUB

CLASS LEADER | ANY OTHER ....

6b. IN THE CIRCUIT? ....

6c. IN THE CONNEXION? ....

7. HOW MANY TIMES DO YOU COME TO THE CHURCH PREMISES EACH WEEK? (on average)

....

8. DO YOU ATTEND

CLASS MEETINGS | BIBLE STUDY GROUP

PRAYER MEETINGS | HEALING MEETINGS

LENT GROUPS

9. DO YOU TAKE PART IN OTHER EVENTS (eg. Fundraising, socials)?

Which? ....

10. DO YOU HAVE ANY CONTACT WITH PEOPLE OF OTHER RELIGIONS

a. as neighbours/friends

b. at work or school/college

c. as a parent

d. through church activities

11. If a. (Neighbours/Friends)

Do you go into each others homes?

Do you go out with them? (eg to shops, school, travel to work)

How well do you know them?

Do you know what religion they belong to?

Do you know anything about their religious beliefs?

Yes What?

No Would you like to?

Have you ever talked about your Christian beliefs with them?

Yes What did you say?

What did they say?

No Why is that?

Do you feel you ought to try and convert them?

Yes Why?

No Why?

Do you feel you would like them better if they were Christians?

Yes Why?

No Why?

What do you think the official Methodist Church teaching is about how Christians should behave in relation to people of other religions?

What is your feeling about this?

Have you read any Church booklets or books about Christian relations with people of other religions?

Yes Which?

How did you get it?

No Did you know there were any?

12. If b. (Work/Education)

How do you feel about working/studying with people of other religions?

Do you know what religion they belong to?

Are there any difficulties at work/school/college because people are Hindus, Sikhs, Muslims etc?

Yes What are they?

What do you think could be done about this?

No Why do you think this is?

Do you know anything about their religious beliefs?

Yes What?

No Would you like to?

Do your workmates/fellow students know you are a practising Christian?

Yes No

Have you ever talked about your Christian beliefs with them?

Yes What did you say?

What did they say?

No Why is that?

Do you feel you <u>ought</u> to try and convert them?

Yes Why?

No Why?

Do you feel you would like them better if they were Christians?

Yes Why?

No Why?

What do you think the official church teaching is about how Christians should behave in relation to people of other religions?

What is your feeling about this?

As a practising Christian, do you think you have anything in common with Hindus, Sikhs, etc. who take their religion seriously?

Yes How?

No What are the differences between you?

13. If c. Through children at school

Do you talk to non-Christian parents at school?

Yes No

Do they have the same concerns about their children's education as you?

Yes What are they?

No Why do you think this is?

Do your children receive teaching about other religions at school?

Yes No

How do you feel about this?

14. If d. (Through church activities)

Are you involved in the provision of any of the following church activities?

PLAYGROUP	MOTHER AND TODDLER GROUP
CUBS	SCOUTS
BROWNIES	WOMENS NETWORK
LUNCH CLUB	

Do any Hindus, Muslims, Sikhs etc attend?

Yes   How did they get involved?

What do you think are the good things about having people of other religions joining in something organised by the church?

Are there any difficulties in having people of other religions joining in?

No   Is this group for church members and friends only?

Would you like people of other religions to join in?

Why?

Why do you think they do not come?

15. Has anything happened to you which has made you think in a different way about Hindus, Sikhs, Muslims, etc. or feel differently towards them?

16. Is there anything we have not talked about that you think is important in Christian relations with people of other religions?

17. How do you think God feels about the people of other religions?

APPENDIX B

THE DOCTRINAL STANDARDS OF THE METHODIST CHURCH

From The Deed of Union in "The Constitutional Practice and Discipline of the Methodist Church Volume 2" (1988) pages 225-7.

The Methodist Church claims and cherishes its place in the Holy Catholic Church which is the Body of Christ. It rejoices in the inheritance of the Apostolic Faith and loyally accepts the fundamental principles of the historic creeds and of the Protestant Reformation. It ever remembers that in the Providence of God Methodism was raised up to spread Scriptural Holiness through the land by the proclamation of the Evangelical Faith and declares its unfaltering resolve to be true to its Divinely appointed mission.

The Doctrines of the Evangelical Faith which Methodism has held from the beginning and still holds are based upon the Divine revelation recorded in the Holy Scriptures. The Methodist Church acknowledges this revelation as the supreme rule of faith and practice. These Evangelical Doctrines to which the Preachers of The Methodist Church both Ministers and Laymen are pledged are contained in Wesley's Notes on the New Testament and the first four volumes of his sermons.

The Notes on the New Testament and the 44 Sermons are not intended to impose a system of formal or speculative theology on Methodist Preachers, but to set up standards of preaching and belief which should secure loyalty to the fundamental truths of the Gospel of Redemption and ensure the continued witness of the Church to the realities of the Christian experience of salvation.

Christ's Ministers in the Church are Stewards in the household of God and Shepherds of His flock. Some are called and ordained to this sole occupation and have a principal and directing part in these great duties but they hold no priesthood differing in kind from that which is common to all the Lord's people and they have no exclusive title to the preaching of the gospel or the care of souls. These ministries are shared with them by others to whom also the Spirit divides His gifts severally as He wills.

It is the universal conviction of the Methodist people that the office of the Christian Ministry depends upon the call of God who bestows the gifts of the Spirit the grace and the fruit which indicate those whom He has chosen.

APPENDIX B (Continued)

Those whom The Methodist Church recognises as called of God and therefore receives into its Ministry shall be ordained by the imposition of hands as expressive of the Church's recognition of the Minister's personal call.

The Methodist Church holds the doctrine of the priesthood of all believers and consequently believes that no priesthood exists which belongs exclusively to a particular order or class of men but in the exercise of its corporate life and worship special qualifications for the discharge of special duties are required and thus the principle of representative selection is recognised.

The Preachers itinerant and lay are examined tested and approved before they are authorised to minister in holy things. For the sake of Church Order and not because of any priestly virtue inherent in the office the Ministers of The Methodist Church are set apart by ordination to the Ministry of the Word and Sacraments.

The Methodist Church recognises two sacraments namely Baptism and the Lord's Supper as of Divine Appointment and of perpetual obligation of which it is the privilege and duty of Members of The Methodist Church to avail themselves.

-oOo-

BIBLIOGRAPHY

Ariarajah, Wesley, "Evangelism and Wesley's Catholicity of Grace" in The Future of the Methodist Theological Traditions, Ed. Douglas Meeks, Abingdon Press, Nashville, 1985.

The Bible and People of Other Faiths; World Council of Churches, Geneva, The Risk Book Series, 1985.

"The understanding and practice of dialogue: its nature, purpose and variations" in Faith in the Midst of Faiths, WCC, ed. Samartha.

Ayling, Stanley, John Wesley; Collins, London, 1979.

The Bible: Revised Standard Version.

Birtwistle, N. Allen, "Methodist Missions" in A History of the Methodist Church in Great Britain Volume 3; Epworth Press, London, 1983.

Bonhoeffer, Dietrich, Letters and Papers from Prison; Collins Fontana Books, 1966 (first published in English by SCM Press 1953).

Board for Mission and Unity of the General Synod of the Church of England, Towards a Theology for Inter-Faith Dialogue; CIO Publishing, London, 1984.

Bouyer, Louis, A History of Christian Spirituality, Volumes I and III; Burns & Oates, Tunbridge Wells, 1968.

British Council of Churches Committee on Relations with People of Other Faiths, Guidelines for Dialogue in Britain; BCC, London, revised edition 1983 (1st edition 1981).

Buber, Martin, I and Thou, translated by Ronald Gregor Smith; T & T Clark, Edinburgh, English translation 2nd (revised) edition 1958, reprinted 1987 (English trans. 1st ed. 1937).

Clark, David, What Future for Methodism?; The National Centre for Christian Communities and Networks, 1988.

Committee for Relations with People of Other Faiths, British Council of Churches, Guidelines on Worship in a Multi-Faith Society; BCC, London, 1983.

Relations with People of Other Faiths: Guidlines for Dialogue in Britain; BCC, London, 1981, Revised Edition 1983.

The Convention for the Promotion of Scriptural Holiness 1875 (Brighton); Garland Publishing Inc., New York and London, 1985.

Cracknell, Kenneth, Towards a New Relationship: Christians and People of Other Faith; Epworth Press, London, 1986.

Why Dialogue?: a first British comment on the WCC Guidelines; Committee for Relations with People of Other Faiths, BCC, London, 1980.

Currie, Robert, Methodism Divided: A Study in the Sociology of Ecumenism; Faber & Faber, London, 1968.

Davies, Rupert, "The People Called Methodists: 'Our Doctrines'" in A History of the Methodist Church in Great Britain Volume 1; Epworth Press, London, 1965.

Davies, Rupert; Rupp, Gordon, (General Eds.), A History of the Methodist Church in Great Britain Volume 1; Epworth Press, London, 1965.

Davies, Rupert; George, Raymond A; Rupp, Gordon, (General Eds.), A History of the Methodist Church in Great Britain Volume 3; Epworth Press, London, 1983.

D'Costa, Gavin, Theology and Religious Pluralism; Basil Blackwell Ltd., Oxford, 1986.

De Alwis, Brian, "Christian Buddhist Dialogue in the Writings of Lynn de Silva", in Dialogue (The Journal of the Ecumenical Institute for Study and Dialogue, Colombo), Vol.X No.1, Jan-May 1983. Synopsis of thesis for Doctor of Theology, University of Michigan, 1982.

De Chardin, Teilhard, Toward the Future; Collins, London, 1975.

The Future of Man; Collins Fount Paperbacks, London, 1964.

The Phenomenon of Man; Collins Fount Paperbacks, London, 1959.

De Silva, Lynn, Editorial Note in Dialogue, Vol.IV No.3, Sep-Dec 1977.

Buddhism: Beliefs and Practices in Sri Lanka: printed in Sri Lanka, 1974.

Dunn, James D. G., Unity and Diversity in the New Testament: An Inquiry into the Character of Earliest Christianity; SCM Press Ltd., London, 1977.

Dunn, James D. G. and Mackey, James, P., New Testament Theology in Dialogue; SPCK, London, 1987.

Dunne, John S., The Reasons of the Heart; SCM Press Ltd., London, 1978.

The Way of All the Earth; Sheldon Press, 1972.

English, Donald, Evangelism Now; The Methodist Church Home Mission Division, London, 1987.

Exley, Richard and Helen, The Missionary Myth; Lutterworth Press, Guildford and London, 1973.

Faith in the City of Birmingham: An examination of problems and opportunities facing a city. Report of a Commission set up by The Bishop's Council of the Diocese of Birmingham, Chairman Sir Richard O'Brien; The Paternoster Press, Exeter, 1988.

Fernando, Antony, Buddhism and Christianity: their inner affinity; Empire Press, Sri Lanka, first published 1981, 2nd ed. 1983.

Fowler, James, "John Wesley's Development in Faith", in The Future of the Methodist Theological Traditions, Ed. Douglas Meeks, Abingdon Press, Nashville, 1985.

Friedman, Maurice, Martin Buber: The Life of Dialogue; The University of Chicago Press Ltd, Chicago and London, 3rd ed. revised, 1976.

Fromm, Erich, You Shall Be As Gods; Jonathan Cape, London, 1967.

Griffiths, Bede, The Marriage of East and West; Collins Fount Paperbacks, London, 1982.

Griffiths, Michael, Ed., Ten Sending Churches; Marc Europe STL Books, Evangelical Missionary Alliance, England, 1985.

Harris, Jeffrey and Jarvis, Peter, Counting to Some Purpose; The Methodist Church Home Mission Division, London, 1979.

Hick, John, The Second Christianity; SCM Press, 1977, 1983.

God Has Many Names; The Macmillan Press Ltd., Papermac, London and Basingstoke, 1980.

Hick, John, Ed., Truth and Dialogue: the relationship between world religions; Studies in Philosophy and Religion 2, Sheldon Press, London, 1974.

Hick, John and Knitter, Paul, Eds., The Myth of Christian Uniqueness; SCM Press Ltd., London, 1988.

Hollenweger, W. J., "Towards an Intercultural History of Christianity"; International Review of Mission Vol. LXXVI No. 304, October 1987, pp.526-556.

Conflict in Corinth and Memoirs of an Old Man; Paulist Press, New York/Ramsey, English translation 1982 by W. J. Hollenweger.

Evangelism Today: Good News or Bone of Contention? Christian Journals Ltd., Belfast, 1976.

Hunter, Alastair, G., Christianity and Other Faiths in Britain; SCM Press Ltd., London 1985.

Israel, S., "Religious Conversion and Interfaith Dialogue", in Discernment: a Christian Journal of Inter-Religious Encounter published by the Committee for Relations with People of Other Faiths of the British Council of Churches, Vol. 3, No. 2, Autumn 1989.

Johnston, William, The Mirror Mind: Spirituality and Transformation; Collins Fount Paperbacks, London, 1983.

Jung, C. G., Selected Writings; introduced by Anthony Storr, Fontana Press, London, 1983.

Memories, Dreams, Reflections; Recorded and edited by Aniela Jaffe, translated by Richard and Clara Wilson; Flamingo/Fontana, London 1983 (first published in Britain 1963).

Kane, Eileen, Doing Your Own Research: basic descriptive research in the social sciences and humanities; Boyars, London, 1985.

Knitter, Paul, No Other Name? A Critical Survey of Christian Attitudes Toward the World Religions; SCM Press Ltd., London, 1985.

Küng, Hans, Christianity and the World Religions, translated by Peter Heinegg; Collins, London, 1987 (original German ed. 1985).

Lochhead, David, The Dialogical Imperative; SCM Press Ltd., London, 1988.

Meeks, Douglas M., Ed., The Future of the Methodist Theological Traditions; Abingdon Press, Nashville, 1985.

The Methodist Church,

The Constitutional Practice and Discipline of the Methodist Church Volumes 1 and 2; Methodist Publishing House, Peterborough, 7th Ed. 1988.

Statements of the Methodist Church on Faith and Order 1933-1983; Methodist Publishing House, Peterborough, 1984.

The Ministry of the People of God: Report presented to the 1986 Methodist Conference by the Faith and Order Committee.

Shall we greet only our own family? Division of Social Responsibility, (Undated, advised published late 1970s).

Sharing in God's Mission, Report Presented to the 1985 Methodist Conference by the Home Mission Division.

The Methodist Recorder, October 1988-April 1989.

Moorhouse, Geoffrey, The Missionaries; Eyre Methuen, London, 1973.

Murphy, Dervla, Tales from Two Cities; Penguin Books, London, 1987.

Neill, Stephen, A History of Christian Missions; Penguin Books, Harmondsworth, Revised edition 1986.

Newbigin, Lesslie, The Open Secret; William B. Eerdmans Publishing Company, Michigan, 1978.

The Finality of Christ; SCM Press Ltd., London, 1969.

Newton, John, C., Jesus in a Multi-Faith Context; Headway (A Movement of Methodists committed to prayer for revival and witness to the Evangelical Faith), 1987 (available from the Cliff College Bookshop).

Ó'Murchú, Diarmuid, MSC, Coping with Change in the Modern World; The Mercier Press, Ltd., Dublin, 1987.

The God Who Becomes Redundant; The Mercier Press Ltd. Fowler Wright Books Ltd., Cork, Leominster, 1986.

Outler, Albert, "A New Future for Wesley Studies" in The Future of the Methodist Theological Traditions, Ed. Douglas Meeks, Abingdon Press, Nashville, 1985.

Parrinder, Geoffrey, What World Religions Teach: Harrap, London, second enlarged edition 1968, reprinted 1977 (first published 1963).

Jesus in the Qur'an, Faber and Faber, London, 1965.

The Christian Debate: Light from the East, Victor Gollancz Ltd., London, 1964.

Pieris, Aloysius, SJ, "Rev. Dr. Lynn A. de Silva: A Tribute"; Supplement to Dialogue, Vol,9, 1-3, Jan-Dec 1982.

Rex, John and Tomlinson, Sally, Colonial Immigrants in a British City: a class analysis; Routledge & Kegan Paul, London, Boston, Melbourne and Henley, 1979.

Robinson, John A. T., Honest to God; SCM Press Ltd., London, 1963.

Russell, Peter, The Awakening Earth: The Global Brain; Ark Paperbacks, London, Melbourne and Henley, first published 1982, reprinted 1985.

Samartha, S. J. Ed., Courage for Dialogue: Ecumenical issues in inter-religious relationships; World Council of Churches, Geneva, 1981.

Faith in the Midst of Faiths: Reflections on Dialogue in Community; World Council of Churches, Geneva, 1977.

Schillebeeckx, Edward, Ministry: A Case for Change; SCM Press Ltd., London, 1981.

Schmidt, Martin, John Wesley: A Theological Biography Vol. 2 John Wesley's Life Mission, Part One; Epworth Press, London, 1971 (first pub. Zurich 1966).

The Young Wesley; Epworth Press, London, 1958.

Smart, Ninian, Religion and the Western Mind; Macmillan, London 1987.

Reasons and Faiths; Routledge and Kegan Paul, London, 1958.

Smith, Wilfred Cantwell, Towards a World Theology; The Macmillan Press Ltd., London, 1981.

The Faith of Other Men; Mentor, Published by The New American Library, New York and The New English Library Ltd., London, 1965.

Strawson, William, "Methodist Theology 1850-1950" in A History of the Methodist Church in Great Britain Volume 3; Epworth Press, London, 1983.

Sub-unit on Dialogue with People of Other Faiths and Ideologies, World Council of Churches, My Neighbour's Faith - and Mine, WCC Geneva, 1986.

Thomas, M. M., Man and the Universe of Faiths; The Christian Literature Society, Madras, India, 1975.

Tillich, Paul, Christianity and the Encounter of the World Religions; Columbia University Press, New York and London, 1963.

Turner, John Munsey, Conflict and Reconciliation: Studies in Methodism and Ecumenism in England 1740-1982; Epworth Press, London, 1985.

"Methodism in England 1900-1932" in A History of the Methodist Church in Great Britain Volume 3: Epworth Press, London, 1983.

Vermes, Gaza, Jesus the Jew; SCM Press Ltd., London, 1973, 1983.

Von Rad, Gerhard, Old Testament Theology Volume I: The Theology of Israel's Historical Traditions; Oliver and Boyd, Edinburgh and London, 1962.

Old Testament Theology Volume II: The Theology of Israel's Prophetic Traditions; SCM Press Ltd., London, 1975 (first published in English in 1965).

Walcot, Kevin, SVD, "Redefining the Boundaries of Mission? Challenges ahead for Missionary Societies", Verbum SVD, Fasciculus 1, Volumen 29, 1988, pp.3-10.

Walton, Heather, with Ward, Robin and Johnson, Mark, A Tree God Planted: black people in British Methodism; Ethnic Minorities in Methodism Working Group, c/o Division of Social Responsibility, 1985.

Warner, Sylvia Townsend, Mr. Fortune's Maggot; Virago, London, 1978 (first published 1927).

Weatherhead, Leslie D., The Christian Agnostic; Hodder & Stoughton, London, 1965.

Key Next Door: and other City Temple Sermons; Hodder & Stoughton, London, 1968 (first ed. 1959).

The Transforming Friendship; London, The Epworth Press, 14th ed. 1932 (first ed. 1928).

Wesley, John, Wesley's Sermons Vols. 2 and 3; John Mason, London, 1851.

John Wesley's Forty-Four Sermons; Epworth, London, first published 1944, 15th impression 1985.

The Letters of John Wesley Volumes V and VIII, Editor J. Telford; the Epworth Press, London, 1931, reprinted 1960.

"A Plain Account of Christian Perfection" in Works XI; Wesleyan Methodist bookroom, Hayman Brothers and Lilly, London. Volume undated; last dated volume 1875 (Vol.VII).

The Journal of John Wesley: A Selection, Ed. Elizabeth Jay; Oxford University Press, Oxford, New York, 1987.

John Wesley: Explanatory Notes Upon the New Testament; Epworth Press, London, 1976 edition, reprinted 1977.

Williams, Colin, John Wesley's Theology Today; Epworth Press, London, 1969, (first published 1960).

Young, Frances and Wilson, Kenneth, Focus on God; Epworth Press, London, 1986.

-oOo-

STUDIEN ZUR INTERKULTURELLEN GESCHICHTE DES CHRISTENTUMS
ETUDES D'HISTOIRE INTERCULTURELLE DU CHRISTIANISME
STUDIES IN THE INTERCULTURAL HISTORY OF CHRISTIANITY

Band 1 Wolfram Weiße: Südafrika und das Antirassismusprogramm. Kirchen im Spannungsfeld einer Rassengesellschaft.

Band 2 Ingo Lembke: Christentum unter den Bedingungen Lateinamerikas. Die katholische Kirche vor den Problemen der Abhängigkeit und Unterentwicklung.

Band 3 Gerd Uwe Kliewer: Das neue Volk der Pfingstler. Religion, Unterentwicklung und sozialer Wandel in Lateinamerika.

Band 4 Joachim Wietzke: Theologie im modernen Indien - Paul David Devanandan.

Band 5 Werner Ustorf: Afrikanische Initivative. Das aktive Leiden des Propheten Simon Kimbangu.

Band 6 Erhard Kamphausen: Anfänge der kirchlichen Unabhängigkeitsbewegung in Südafrika. Geschichte und Theologie der äthiopischen Bewegung. 1880-1910.

Band 7 Lothar Engel: Kolonialismus und Nationalismus im deutschen Protestantismus in Namibia 1907-1945. Beiträge zur Geschichte der deutschen evangelischen Mission und Kirche im ehemaligen Kolonial- und Mandatsgebiet Südwestafrika.

Band 8 Pamela M. Binyon: The Concepts of "Spirit" and "Demon". A Study in the use of different languages describing the same phenomena.

Band 9 Neville Richardson: The World Council of Churches and Race Relations. 1960 to 1969.

Band 10 Jörg Müller: Uppsala II. Erneuerung in der Mission. Eine redaktionsgeschichtliche Studie und Dokumentation zu Sektion II der 4. Vollversammlung des Ökumenischen Rates der Kirchen, Uppsala 1968.

Band 11 Hans Schöpfer: Theologie und Gesellschaft. Interdisziplinäre Grundlagenbibliographie zur Einführung in die befreiungs- und polittheologische Problematik: 1960-1975.

Band 12 Werner Hoerschelmann: Christliche Gurus. Darstellung von Selbstverständnis und Funktion indigenen Christseins durch unabhängige charismatisch geführte Gruppen in Südindien.

Band 13 Claude Schaller: L'Eglise en quête de dialogue. Vergriffen.

Band 14 Theo Tschuy: Hundert Jahre kubanischer Protestantismus (1868-1961). Versuch einer kirchengeschichtlichen Darstellung.

Band 15 Werner Korte: Wir sind die Kirchen der unteren Klassen. Entstehung, Organisation und gesellschaftliche Funktionen unabhängiger Kirchen in Afrika.

Band 16 Arnold Bittlinger: Pabst und Pfingstler. Der römisch katholisch-pfingstliche Dialog und seine ökumenische Relevanz.

Band 17 Ingemar Lindén: The Last Trump. An historico-genetical study of some important chapters in the making and development of the Seventh-day Adventist Church.

Band 18 Zwinglio Dias: Krisen und Aufgaben im brasilianischen Protestantismus. Eine Studie zu den sozialgeschichtlichen Bedingungen und volkspädagogischen Möglichkeiten der Evangelisation.

Band 19 Mary Hall: A quest for the liberated Christian, Examined on the basis of a mission, a man and a movement as agents of liberation.

Band 20 Arturo Blatezky: Sprache des Glaubens in Lateinamerika. Eine Studie zu Selbstverständnis und Methode der "Theologie der Befreiung".

Band 21 Anthony Mookenthottam: Indian Theological Tendencies. Approaches and problems for further research as seen in the works of some leading Indian theologicans.

Band 22 George Thomas: Christian Indians and Indian Nationalism 1885-1950. An Interpretation in Historical and Theological Perspectives.

Band 23 Essiben Madiba: Evangélisation et Colonisation en Afrique: L'Héritage scolaire du Cameroun (1885-1965).

Band 24 Katsumi Takizawa: Reflexionen über die universale Grundlage von Buddhismus und Christentum.

Band 25 S.W. Sykes (editor): England and Germany. Studies in theological diplomacy.

Band 26 James Haire: The Character and Theological Struggle of the Church in Halmahera, Indonesia, 1941-1979.

Band 27 David Ford: Barth and God's Story. Biblical Narrative and the Theological Method of Karl Barth in the Church Dogmatics.

Band 28 Kortright Davis: Mission for Carribean Change. Carribean Development As Theological Enterprice.

Band 29 Origen V. Jathanna: The Decisiveness of the Christ-Event and the Universality of Christianity in a world of Religious Plurality. With Special Reference to Hendrik Kraemer and Alfred George Hogg as well as to William Ernest Hocking and Pandipeddi Chenchiah.

Band 30 Joyce V. Thurman: New Wineskins. A Study of the House Church Movement.

Band 31 John May: Meaning, Consensus and Dialogue in Buddhist-Christian-Communication. A study in the Construction of Meaning.

Band 32 Friedhelm Voges: Das Denken von Thomas Chalmers im kirchen- und sozialgeschichtlichen Kontext.

Band 33 George MacDonald Mulrain: Theology in Folk Culture. The Theological Significance of Haitian Folk Religion.

Band 34 Alan Ford: The Protestant Reformation in Ireland, 1590-1641. 2. unveränderte Auflage.

Band 35 Harold Tonks: Faith, Hope and Decision-Making. The Kingdom of God and Social Policy-Making. The Work of Arthur Rich of Zürich.

Band 36 Bingham Tembe: Integrationismus und Afrikanismus. Zur Rolle der kirchlichen Unabhängigkeitsbewegung in der Auseinandersetzung um die Landfrage und die Bildung der Afrikaner in Südafrika, 1880-1960.

Band 37 Kingsley Lewis: The Moravian Mission in Barbados 1816-1886. A Study of the Historical Context and Theological Signifcance of a Minority Church Among an Oppressed People.

Band 38 Ulrich M. Dehn: Indische Christen in der gesellschaftlichen Verantwortung. Eine theologische und religionssoziologische Untersuchung politischer Theologie im gegenwärtigen Indien.

Band 39 Walter J. Hollenweger (Ed.): Pentecostal Research in Europe: Problems, Promises and People. Proceedings from the Pentecostal Research Conference at the University of Birmingham (England) April 26th to 29th 1984.

Band 40 P. Solomon Raj: A Christian Folk-Religion in India. A Study of the Small Church Movement in Andhra Pradesh, with a Special Reference to the Bible Mission of Devadas.

Band 41 Karl-Wilhelm Westmeier: Reconciling Heaven and earth: The Transcendental Enthusiasm and Growth of an Urban Protestant Community, Bogota, Colombia.

Band 42 George A. Hood: Mission Accomplished? The English Presbyterian Mission in Lingtung, South China. A Study of the Interplay between Mission Methods and their Historical Context.

Band 43 Emmanuel Yartekwei Lartey: Pastoral Counselling in Inter-Cultural Perspective: A Study of some African (Ghanaian) and Anglo-American viewes on human existence and councelling.

Band 44 Jerry L. Sandidge: Roman Catholic/Pentecostal Dialogue (1977-1982): A Study in Developing Ecumenism.

Band 45 Friedeborg L. Müller: The History of German Lutheran Congregations in England, 1900-1950.

Band 46 Roger B. Edrington: Everyday Men: Living in a Climate of Unbelief.

Band 47 Bongani Mazibuko: Education in Mission/Mission in Education. A Critical Comparative Study of Selected Approaches.

Band 48 Jochanan Hesse (Ed.): Mitten im Tod - vom Leben umfangen. Gedenkschrift für Werner Kohler.

Band 49 Elisabeth A. Kasper: Afrobrasilianische Religion. Der Mensch in der Beziehung zu Natur, Kosmos und Gemeinschaft im Candomblé - eine tiefenpsychologische Studie.

Band 50 Charles Chikezie Agu: Secularization in Igboland. Socio-religious Change and its Challenges to the Church Among the Igbo.

Band 51 Abraham Adu Berinyuu: Pastoral Care to the Sick in Africa. An Approach to Transcultural Pastoral Theology.

Band 52 Boo-Woong Yoo: Korean Pentecostalism. Its History and Theology.

Band 53 Roger H. Hooker: Themes in Hinduism and Christianity. A Comparative Study.

Band 54 Jean-Daniel Plüss: Therapeutic and Prophetic Narratives in Worship. A Hermeneutic Study of Testimonies and Visions. Their Potential Significance for Christian Worship and Secular Society.

Band 55 John Mansford Prior: Church and Marriage in an Indonesian Village. A Study of Customary and Church Marriage among the Ata Lio of Central Flores, Indonesia, as a Paradigm of the Ecclesial Interrelationship between village and Institutional Catholicism.

Band 56 Werner Kohler: Umkehr und Umdenken. Grundzüge einer Theologie der Mission (herausgegeben von Jörg Salaquarda).

Band 57 Martin Maw: Visions of India. Fulfilment Theology, the Aryan Race Theory, & the Work of British Protestant Missionaries in Victorian India.

Band 58 Aasulv Lande: Meiji Protestantism in History and Historiography. A Comparative Study of Japanese and Western Interpretation of Early Protestantism in Japan.

Band 59 Enyi Ben Udoh: Guest Christology. An interpretative view of the christological problem in Africa.

Band 60 Peter Schüttke-Scherle: From Contextual to Ecumenical Theology? A Dialogue between Minjung Theology and 'Theology after Auschwitz'.

Band 61 Michael S. Northcott: The Church and Secularisation. Urban Industrial Mission in North East England.

Band 62 Daniel O'Connor: Gospel, Raj and Swaraj. The Missionary Years of C. F. Andrews 1904-14.

Band 63 Paul D. Matheny: Dogmatics and Ethics. The Theological Realism and Ethics of Karl Barth's Church Dogmatics.

Band 64 Warren Kinne: A People's Church? The Mindanao-Sulu Church Debacle.

Band 65 Jane Collier: The culture of economism. An exploration of barriers to faith-as-praxis.

Band 66 Michael Biehl: Der Fall Sadhu Sundar Singh. Theologie zwischen den Kulturen.

Band 67 Brian C. Castle: Hymns: The Making and Shaping of a Theology for the Whole People of God. A Comparison of the Four Last Things in Some English and Zambian Hymns in Intercultural Perspective.

Band 68 Jan A. B. Jongeneel (Ed.): Experiences of the Spirit. Conference on Pentecostal and Charismatic Research in Europe at Utrecht University 1989 .

Band 69 William S. Campbell: Paul's Gospel in an Intercultural Context. Jew and Gentile in the Letter to the Romans.

Band 70 Lynne Price: Interfaith Encounter and Dialogue. A Methodist Pilgrimage.